PROTECTION CHARMS

For my father, Hamraz Ahsan,
with love and gratitude always.

Published by OH!
An imprint of Welbeck Publishing Group Limited
20 Mortimer Street
London W1T 3JW

ISBN 978-1-78739-592-3

A CIP catalogue record for this book is available from the British Library.

Printed in Spain

10 9 8 7 6 5 4 3 2 1

PROTECTION CHARMS

HARNESS YOUR ENERGY FORCE TO GUARD AGAINST PSYCHIC ATTACK

TANIA AHSAN

Contents

Introduction

Do you ever feel as though life has become more combative and difficult to navigate, with angry people on the news, social media trolls and even your own family and friends being more sensitive to the slightest perceived criticism or disagreement? Does this represent a true analysis of life in the early 21st century, or is every generation convinced that their society is worse than those that came before?

If we are to get upset about the terrible things that are happening in the world, we must also be fair and appreciate the good things. Our medical knowledge is far more advanced than it was in earlier centuries. Our ideas about social justice and human rights are much improved. Our desire for good environmental practices is now gaining ground, with calls from the public to end devastating climate change. We have things to applaud and celebrate.

However, the fantastically fast technological growth that has taken place means that we now have an intense connection with the world around us, which lets in both positive and negative ideas. There is an oft-quoted saying that 'energy flows where attention goes'. Regrettably the algorithms of much of our online life are also set by that principle, so if you give your attention to negative news, you will find that these are the things that appear more and more on your news and social media feeds. If you concentrate on puppies and kittens then you are

energy flows where
attention goes

more likely to be shown those. It is a good idea to consciously decide what you look at and listen to. However, as much as we would like to live in a pleasant, positive world, at times we must interact with terrible news, thoughts and, indeed, behaviour. So, how can you best navigate the ills of modern life?

I have edited mind-body-spirit magazines and books for more than two decades now, and this book is a distillation of the energy work I have learned from a number of different spiritual practitioners and traditions. All the techniques here have been tried and tested over several years. However, what works for me may not work for you. All energy work is an individual process, and if something doesn't feel right, trust yourself and move on to another practice that may suit your energy body better.

A note on magick (the extra 'k' in this spelling of magick differentiates it from the magic of illusions, card tricks and rabbits in hats): I self-identify as a pagan and a witch, but I do not follow one specific tradition. As such, I have an unapologetically eclectic approach to magickal work. Therefore, in this book you will find energy practices and magickal charms for protection from all over the globe. You may find that one tradition attracts you more than others; it is my belief that we are all children from one divine source and so should be free to seek spiritual guidance and love in any culture where we feel most at home.

This book is about protection charms and relates to the objects of power that you can create once you understand the energetic principles that govern our world. The word 'charm' has Latin origins in the word *carmen*, meaning 'song' or 'chant'. Charm, in its medieval usage, meant a magickal incantation, a written spell or magickal recipe. It was also taken to mean putting someone or something under a spell or enchantment.

Our modern, secular use of the word is for the little tokens of jewellery that women wear on bracelets – each one representative of a particular event or memento. Even this usage has roots in ancient practices to ward off evil and attract good fortune. Stones and small trinkets have been found from the Neolithic era (4000BCE–1500BCE), which suggests that Neolithic tribes carried such items with them as good luck tokens, perhaps to help in hunts at a time when life must have seemed difficult and brutish without some supernatural help. This book takes on that meaning of an amulet or talisman as an object to concentrate energetic, magickal intent. All charms are either to protect against bad luck or evil influences (apotropaic), or to attract good luck and manifest the best outcomes.

Throughout the world, in myriad cultures and religions, and in different eras, we find objects imbued with these protective powers. Examples include the witch bottles that have been found buried in hearths throughout the UK, Ireland and the USA; the *tawiz* (amulet) worn by many in the Indian sub-continent; the *tcherot* (meaning 'message', to refer to talismanic notes hidden inside the amulet) of the Tuareg people of northern Africa; and the Yansheng coins of China. There are many more all over the world. Guarding against ill fortune and bringing forth luck has been a key concern for people around the world. Even as we move into more secular times, we retain a belief in luck and, on occasion, even the most cynical among us will avoid certain practices said to be unlucky.

Here we will look primarily at protection charms and the energetic magick that keeps us protected in our daily lives. This starts with preparing yourself and your space to ensure the optimum conditions for beginning to work with charms. You will discover the basics of your energy make-up and how to work safely with energy as well as the principles of repelling and attracting outcomes. You will also learn rituals to keep your energy clear regularly, and how to nourish yourself so that you are in the best place to do this work.

Then we will look at how to use specific symbols for specific outcomes, and you will learn how to trust your own intuition when preparing a charm to be worn, displayed or used in a ritual.

Finally, we will look at how to ensure that your charms continue to work and how to 'troubleshoot' any that are not working. The information in this book will enable you to understand how protective charms work and learn how to make ones that will work for you alone.

This can be extremely rewarding work, not just for the results you see, but because you begin to understand your own energetic make-up much better. You will start to recognize the people and situations that drain you of energy and can take steps to ensure that the effect on you is minimal. You will also begin to fortify and balance yourself so that you feel alive and present in every moment. A daily practice of magickal work can give you a tremendous sense of achievement and allow you to step into your personal power.

Introduction

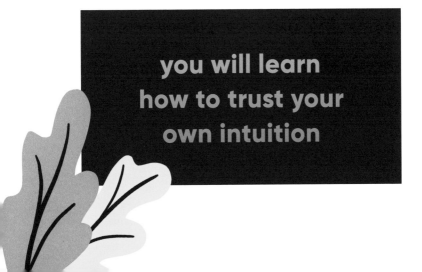

you will learn how to trust your own intuition

1

Energetic

Hygiene

Before you can begin any magickal work, you need to cleanse your energy and that of the space in which you will be creating your charms. This is not just about physical hygiene; it is cleansing the invisible energies around you and your home. Without this vitally important step in the process, your charms and magickal intent will not be pure and can be tainted by unhelpful thought forms, stagnant energies and negative experiences. At best, this will result in no potency in your spellwork and, at worst, having the opposite effect to the one you are seeking. However, once you begin a regular practice, you will find that your energy and that of your space starts to strengthen in its protective abilities and you can very quickly enter in the right state of mind for magick. In this section we look at the ingredients, tools and practices used for energetic cleansing.

Before
you start

IS THE MOON PHASE IMPORTANT?

Many witches in the western tradition say that it is best to attract on a waxing moon phase and repel on a waning. However, because the charms you will create work on the energy matrix on which we all operate in our daily lives, there is no need to wait for a waning moon to begin your energy cleansing routine. The word routine is the most important here as you will need to make a regular time to do this energy cleansing. I recommend a full run-through of the energy clearing given on pages 40-42, followed by the 'top-up' suggestion for testing energy in your home on pages 48.

SEASONAL CHARMS

The herbs and invocations you use will differ according to where in the world you are and also what time of year it is. For example, say you live in Australia and are about to sit some exams – a small pillow of lemon myrtle kept in your bag will help you retain mental focus when studying or about to sit down at your desk to do the tests. It is important to read up on the herbs and flora of your particular part of the world, as the most powerful charms are those embedded in the earth of where you live.

DEITIES AND ANCESTORS

You have guides who will help you by protecting you from harm. However, you have to appeal to them by creating an energetic bridge. You should look for signs in your daily life. It may be that a particular image draws you in or you have always felt drawn to a particular deity, perhaps one not in your own spiritual tradition. Go with your instinct and note well the corresponding colours, symbols and incense associated with particular gods. Your charms will be all the more powerful if you ensure that you build a magickal practice that is consistent and feels intuitively right.

OTHER PEOPLE

If you live with others, you may find yourself limited to some degree in what you can do. For example, your partner might find the smell of sage burning is not to their liking, or your children might interrupt you when you're clearing your own energy. It can be very hard to find the right time to engage in energetic cleansing but, just as we find the time to shower, bathe and wash our hands, we must find the time to clear our energy. It may well be that the only thing you have the time and opportunity to do is a visualization for yourself – this is still better than nothing (you can find one on page 20). Even 5 minutes a day spent in such a way will help you begin your magickal protective work.

If you live with others – and have the kind of relationship that enables you to do this – try telling those who share your space what you're doing. You may find that you are the butt of a few jokes, but many people are curious about these subjects and certainly we can all feel the strange tension in a room where a fight has just occurred. You may just be able to get them to open their minds to the idea that an energetically clean space will serve all who live in it better.

Energetic Hygiene

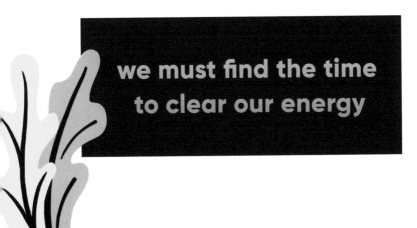

we must find the time to clear our energy

Toolkit for
energy cleansing

SALTS
see the list opposite for the different
varieties and their effects

A BESOM
or natural wood brush

A BOWL
used just for ritual purposes

A SMUDGE STICK
or incense

SELENITE CRYSTAL
(optional)

SALT CLEARING

SEA SALT
for general use

This has the greatest link to water and is good for emotional balance. Use when clearing a room after a fight.

TABLE SALT
for general use

This is the most processed salt you can buy; however, it is cheap and widely available. Use in larger rooms.

HIMALAYAN SALT
for attracting love

A lovely pale pink colour, it is used in rituals for attracting love. A higher iron content makes it good for protection.

BLACK SALT
for personal protection

There are a number of different black salts:

Witch's salt

Made by mixing together the scrapings from the bottom of your ritual cauldron or cast-iron pot, the relevant herbs and salt. This is not edible but is great for expelling any negative energy around you. Carrying a pouch of this is a good all-round protection.

Kala namak

A sulphurous-smelling salt used in cooking and in Ayurveda in the Indian sub-continent, this is handy in edible charms and can be ingested.

Hawaiian lava salt

Made with sea salt and volcanic charcoal, this salt most represents the union of all four elements in its purest form and is a powerful salt to use in personal protection rituals.

Energetic Hygiene

Your energy make-up

You are not just your physical body; you also comprise energy bodies that radiate outwards. These interact with one another and enable you to connect on different levels with the world and those around you. Have you ever been on a crowded commuter train? Squashed up against strangers, our instinct is to try and retain personal space through the positioning of our body and by avoiding eye contact. Yet, even if we are not being physically touched by anyone in the carriage, the feeling of being in such close proximity to others is unpleasant. We hate it when people we have not invited to be intimate with us are in our personal space. This is because, just as you wouldn't want your skin to be touched unless it was by someone you wanted to touch you, the field of subtle energies around you also reacts and alerts you to feelings of being 'invaded' if someone is standing within your personal space. This is more pleasantly seen when we take an immediate liking to someone for no logical reason; we are experiencing their energy field and reacting well to it.

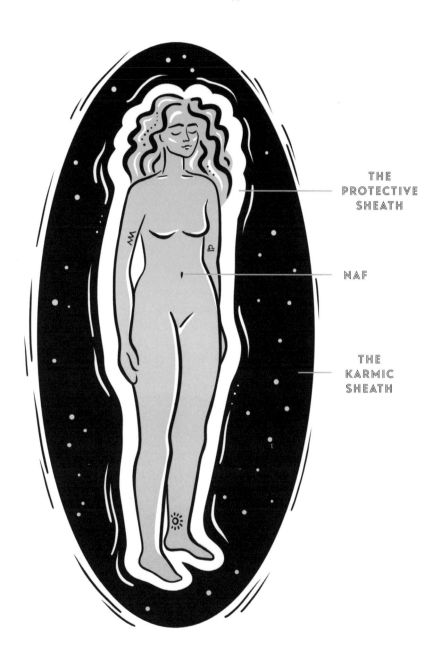

THE
PROTECTIVE
SHEATH

NAF

THE
KARMIC
SHEATH

Energetic Hygiene

The aura's
sheaths

You are surrounded by something called an aura. This is comprised of subtle energy bodies that delineate where you end, and the world begins, greater than the boundary of your skin. Different spiritual traditions, such as theosophy, Tantra and Sufism, for example, have different ideas of how those bodies and your aura are ordered, and how it all works. Many use the theosophical seven-layer system for ordering the aura. However, for the purposes of this book, we will simply look at two elements of your energy make-up.

karma is the experiences we have over many lives

KARMIC SHEATH

Within your aura, at its most outward extent, is the karmic sheath in which you hold a record of all that you've said, done and believed across each of your lives. Karma is the experiences we have over many lives. As corporeal beings (meaning we are in a physical body), in each life, we take on a variety of different roles and behaviours in order to gain the fullest experience of our corporeality. All of these are then stored in our aura as a permanent record that we carry around with us until we finish fully with manifest reality, and return to the creation energy from which we were formed at the start of time.

This is not 'cleansed' when you clear your aura; it is the sum of your spirit's experiences and requires no cleaning or expunging. It is also the field that draws different experiences to us.

PROTECTIVE SHEATH

What we are actually cleaning is not the part of the aura that remains after our deaths, but the protective sheath, which represents the energy of our current day-to-day life. This is not permanent and changes moment by moment. It is the energy layer closest to our physical bodies. It is affected by everything from our hormones and moods, to external events and our beliefs about ourselves and others. This sheath is also the seat of our intuition, and so if it is not strong and well-cleared of problematic influences, it can affect our ability to judge the world around us. It can also leave us open to psychic attack when our beliefs make it porous and susceptible to forming outside circuits.

Energetic Hygiene

HOW TO CLEANSE YOUR SHEATH

The easiest and most convenient way to cleanse your protective sheath is with visualization. While you can do this practice anywhere – and indeed I'd encourage you to do this on your morning commute if you have one – it is best done initially at a time and place where you will not be disturbed.

1. Take three deep breaths in and out of your nose.

2. You can either close your eyes or, when you become better at visualizing in spite of visual stimuli, you can do this with your eyes open: imagine a shaft of white light coming down from the sky (or roof if you're indoors) and entering through the top of your head.

3. As it moves down it circulates around your entire body. This white light clears all the muddiness or stains in your protective sheath and brightens your whole energy outline. It also reaches under and over your feet, together with your front and back.

4. You can breathe into this field of energy and in fact it feels clearer, as though the air around you is cleaner and fresher.

5. Once you have that visualization clear in your mind, seal it as if it is a bubble you are inside.

6. Give thanks to whichever deity you connect with or simply to universal energy for helping you in this way. Then go about your day, knowing you have strengthened your protective sheath.

WAYS TO PROTECT THE SHEATH

- Keep a diary of emotions and note who you've seen or spoken to when you feel bad about yourself or in general – always do the visualization whenever you're about to see that person or when you've come from meeting with them.

- Always take a salt bath after a fight or confrontation – whether that is in real life, with your family, or online. The different types of salt are listed on page 15 – just add a couple of generous handfuls to a warm bath (ideally avoid using table salt unless you really have nothing else as it is heavily processed and therefore a bit too harsh on the skin). Remember to either submerge the crown of your head or cup your hands and pass the salt water over your head. Shower and moisturize afterwards so that the salt doesn't dry out your skin.

- You can also perform an egg ritual to cleanse the protective sheath. Take a free-range organic egg and gently roll it from the top of your head over the whole length of your body. Rub it around your belly and across your genitals. Then crack the egg into the toilet and flush it away, visualizing all the 'dirt' in your protective sheath as having been transferred to the egg and flushed away.

Energetic Hygiene

Naf: your centre
of healing

In terms of your energy make-up, your stomach is the most vital organ. I call this point of energy 'naf', which is the Persian word for belly button. The English word 'navel' comes from an old Anglo-Saxon word *nafela*. The Greek word for navel is *bembix*, which literally means 'whirlpool', hinting at the way that the movement of chakras has been described by almost all energetic medicine practitioners. Most interestingly of all, the root word for 'umbilical' in Latin is *umbo*, which means the boss of a shield – the rounded, strongest part of a shield.

Have you ever said, 'I don't have the stomach for it'? This means that you are repelled by an action; you fear it. Queen Elizabeth I of England said,' I know I have the body of a weak and feeble woman, but I have the heart and stomach of a king.' This is a good indication of how far our strength lies in this part of our bodies.

In several cultures, the belly button was closely associated with sex and fertility, because it was thought to resemble the vagina. This association led to much modern censoring of the female navel.

Indian soothsayers believed that a woman with a deep belly button would be much loved by her husband. Shallow belly buttons were also good news, as they indicated a woman who was generally lucky.

It is not just the human body that has this centre of energy: many believe there are places on Earth that serve the same function in physical geography. In Abrahamic religions, Jerusalem is considered the navel of the world. Cuzco, an important city in Peru, is named for the Quechua (Inca) word for navel. The axis mundi (or centre of the Earth) is said to be the place of connection between Heaven and Earth. For the Sioux that is the black hills in the Great Plains of North America. Mount Kailash in Tibet serves the same purpose in many religions of the Indian sub-continent. Likewise, Mount Fuji is the axis mundi of Japan.

NAVEL-GAZING

The term 'navel-gazing' is often used in a disparaging way to suggest someone who is far too interested in themselves or in a particular issue to look up and see the bigger picture. However, it actually derives from a spiritual practice common in both ancient Greek and Indian cultures. The Greeks called this *omphaloskepsis*, a contemplation of the navel that was used as an aid to meditation and communion with divinity. Yogis also undertake this practice and activate the Manipura or Nabhi chakra (energy centre) to gain insight into the nature of the Universe. This chakra centre has, in the Western alternative spiritual tradition, been associated with power and purpose. It is considered the seat of will. However, other commentators have attributed it with even greater powers. Swami Brahmavidya, writing in *The Science of Self Knowledge* (1922), revealed the ultimate importance of this energy centre for protection work:

'Another great key I will give you is to be found by the contemplation of the Manipur Lotus, which is in the navel, or thereabouts. By contemplating this centre, you will be able to enter and go into another person's body, take possession of that person's mind, and cause him to think and to do what you want him to do; you will obtain the power of transmuting metals, of healing the sick and afflicted, and of seership.'

Energetic Hygiene

HOW TO PROTECT THE NAF

1. The first principle is to keep your belly button physically clean – so get rid of that fluff!

2. Then you should anoint it once a week with consecrated oil. Take a dish of olive or coconut oil and blow into it three times saying aloud each time, 'I bless you'. You can add any deity invocation that is appropriate for your particular practice or beliefs.

3. Using the middle finger (this is the digit associated with Saturn) of your right hand, dip your finger into the oil and rub it into your belly button in a clockwise direction.

4. If you are feeling energetically assaulted, and are unable to sit and do a ritual with oil, you can also visualize a golden light entering at the top of your head and then coming out of your belly button to form a large sparkling shield that covers all of your midriff. This will help stop any energetic assaults or psychic attack you might come across. Always remember to thank universal energy or the deity you worship when undertaking these visualizations.

To protect your naf in other ways you can:

- Draw the most appropriate charm in Part 2 (pages 82-113) on a piece of paper, burn it in the fireproof bowl you use for ritual purposes and apply the ash around your belly button for protection.

- Wear silk. It is an easy way to protect your belly button when worn as a cummerbund or camisole inside your everyday clothes. If you are vegan and not able to wear silk, try the ash or oil anointments as above.

- Place your hand at your belly button any time you feel that you're in the company of those who wish you harm. It will provide a measure of comfort and will calm your fear. It will also signal energetically that you are closed off to psychic attack.

Protecting
your energy

Whenever I give talks on witchcraft, I am always asked about curses and how to protect against them. I explain that it is extremely rare to be the recipient of a curse unless you have agreed on some level to be receptive to it. This is because a curse is like an electrical circuit – it needs unimpeded flow in order to work. If you block or break it, it is impossible for it to work. You leave yourself open to it by expecting that this is what is happening to you. Many get upset when they hear this, thinking that I am blaming them for their own misfortune. This is to misunderstand what I'm saying: we are powerful beings, but we can leave ourselves open to negativity by allowing it into our lives through not maintaining good thinking or energy practices.

Here are some things you can do to ensure you repel negative energy or 'curses':

- Do not dwell on the idea of curses or cursing;

- Try to think well of people – even those you dislike;

- Regularly do the practices in the next section on energy clearing (see pages 32-49).

Energetic Hygiene

You should also stay intuitively alert. There are times I won't take a certain route home from work, even in broad daylight, simply because I have a feeling I shouldn't. I always find there is a reason for why I did not do this, such as an act of violence or a disruption of some kind along that route that day. I am not able to predict what it will be, but I do listen whenever I am told energetically to be elsewhere.

Quite apart from the problems that other people might pose in the form of curses or physical attacks, you yourself are a source of danger if you don't understand the energy work you are doing.

CONQUERING FEAR

I once visited a woman who ran a goddess group and in her kitchen she had a huge mirror on one wall that was etched with the Sri Yantra. This is a mystical design that represents the union between male and female divinity – the god Shiv and the goddess Shakti. It has many layers of meaning and is one of the most powerful yantras used in the Indian Tantric traditions. To put it on a mirror was a terrible idea since this creates a portal through which any number of entities and energies are welcome to enter. I used mudras (hand gestures) to protect myself while in that space, but I didn't leave. The mudras only had a small effect and I was then horribly ill for about six weeks. A lot of my illness was from my own fears regarding the yantra on a mirror. I knew from my knowledge of these powerful diagrams that this was a bad idea, but I allowed the fear of it having a negative effect to become a self-fulfilling prophecy.

This example shows how easy it is to allow your own fears to manifest negative outcomes in your life. You must guard against worrying and giving any truck to fear-based thoughts.

Often, when you are working with energy – especially in meditation – you may find yourself feeling light-headed, and you may even suffer flu-like symptoms. This is due to a lack of grounding. Before and after any energy work, we need to ensure we ground ourselves back into the real world. The way you can do this very simply is by putting your hands, with your palms down, on the top of your thighs and keeping them there for a few moments. As I mentioned before, we are almost like circuits, so whenever you do anything with your palms exposed, energy moves through and out of them. If you want to break the circuit and ground yourself, cutting off the flow through your palms is a good way to do this.

You should also always ensure that any sitting meditations you do are with your feet flat on the ground. Avoid lying-down meditations until you are more comfortable with energy work.

Energetic Hygiene

before and after any energy work, we need to ensure we ground ourselves back into the real world

Energetic principles

Have you ever had a day when everything has gone well? Your commute was great, every decision you made just felt right, and you had oodles of good luck at every turn. Wouldn't it be terrific to have that sort of day on tap all the time? Well, you can.

We all have the ability to bring good things into our lives and to avoid the bad. There are a number of practical actions you can take to ensure you are in the right mindset for attracting the good and repelling the bad. Just be aware that even if something is a mental process, that makes it no less practical and useful. Thoughts are real things and manifest as real allies or obstacles in your life.

we all have the ability to bring good things into our lives and to avoid the bad

REPELLING

- Don't 'curse-speak' – this means don't say things you don't want to manifest, even jokingly. 'I'm such a moron!' 'As if he would ever want me...' 'I'm always broke.'

- Don't base your humour on depreciation of either yourself or anyone else. You may think it is worth it for the laughs, but you are again – as per the principle above – 'curse-speaking'.

- Never do something a second time that you hated the first. Sometimes we have to do things we hate, such as attend funerals, but if you can help it, avoid the things that make you unhappy.

- If you experience a thought, word or deed from either yourself or someone else that feels bad to you, say 'I cancel that' or immediately imagine that it has evaporated on an invisible shield you have all around you emanating from your belly.

ATTRACTING

- Bathe regularly. This may seem a very personal thing to say, but if you want to attract the best to you, make sure you spend time regularly washing the dirt of the day off you so that your energy stays physically clear.

- Meditate. Whichever form you use – whether the physical form of yoga or the sound form of chanting or just concentrating on your breath – meditation is what causes your energy to become attractive to the beauty in the world.

- Be kind. Animals, plants and other humans can sense when someone means them well. The kinder you become, the better you attract loveliness to you.

- Be resilient. If things don't immediately turn out the way you want, be patient and stick with doing the principles above, especially concentrating on feeling gratitude for what you do have.

Energetic Hygiene

Over the next two pages, we look in more detail at what you can do to become an attracting force for good.

GRATITUDE

You will probably have heard how important it is to express gratitude in order to manifest better outcomes in philosophies such as the Law of Attraction. If you regularly give thanks for the blessings in your life, you will find those blessings increase. However, it is also important in order to strengthen your protective sheath. Lack of gratitude or constant complaining can cause fissures and gaps in that protective energy layer and manifest as inflammation in the body that can cause illnesses or mental distress. Certainly I'm sure we can all attest to feeling better when we've spent time in the company of someone who makes us laugh rather than someone who complains about all the terrible things that have happened to them or are likely to happen. Of course, we should have compassion for people as we can't always have a joyful experience of life, but if you find that you are also looping into complaint rather than gratitude, make a shift and remind yourself of everything that is great in your life.

POSITIVE THOUGHTS

Thought forms are also important in retaining a clear channel for manifesting the good and repelling the bad. If you find yourself having negative thoughts about any aspect of your day, say to yourself, 'I cancel this thought. I am having a great day.' All magick works on the power of belief – some have a greater trust in their ability to manifest than others. Be like them and retain a strong sense of faith made real through good, positive thoughts. Here is an example: have you ever been in an office where everyone does that good-natured eyeroll about how great it is when Friday rolls around? Don't engage with this seemingly harmless group mentality. If you do, you will be telling yourself that you hate your job enough to want Friday to come around. Wouldn't you rather love your job so much that you forget entirely what day it is? Wouldn't it be great not to have the Sunday-evening blues? Well, watch your thoughts and your words to avoid those unthinking cues of unhappiness, and you'll soon be on your way to attracting the most incredible experience of daily life.

GUT HEALTH

Finally, the naf is also important in this work as you will know 'in your gut' if a particular outcome is right for you. Theodore Zeldin in his classic book *An Intimate History of Humanity* (1994) writes: 'It used to be believed that the stomach was the seat of the emotions, but what actually happens in the stomach when fear is felt – and one vomits, or has butterflies, or has any of the many disabling sensations that the stomach can produce – only became clear in the 1950s.' He gives us the example of a Professor Stewart Wolf of Oklahoma who, over several years, studied Tom, a hospital worker who had burned his oesophagus as a child and could only ingest food through a hole in his stomach. Wolf found that '... the stomach revealed itself as far more interesting than the heart, the supposed seat of emotion, whose monotonous pumping has nothing particularly human about it.' Wolf could see waterfalls of acid when Tom was fearful and anxiety would turn his stomach pale. The stomach even bled and attempted to destroy its own lining when it felt Tom's circumstances were too hard to bear.

If all energy can be split into love or fear (as many spiritual teachers say) then appeasement of the stomach must feature large in your work – you must take it from fear into love. Attune yourself to the workings of your stomach. Good digestion, perhaps with the aid of the right probiotics and prebiotics, if suitable for you personally, must be a key component of your preparation for energy work.

Energetic Hygiene

Energy
clearing

In the last section we looked at some elements of how to cleanse your energy, protect yourself from psychic attack and attract good things. Now we are going to look at how to keep our energy clear on a daily basis in order to create powerful charms to protect us.

The greatest, and most difficult, act you can perform for your energetic ablutions is to check your thoughts. You can have as many cleansing ritual baths as you like, but if your thoughts are not monitored to avoid 'ill-speaking' then it will have no effect. You must reframe your thoughts into higher ones.

For example, you may feel annoyed about someone barging past you in the street. Your impulse might be to become angry, to call the person names in your head (or out loud!), and you will feel the adrenaline coursing through your veins as your brain signals that you are about to have a row with someone. That 'fight or flight' instinct kicks in almost without you consciously becoming aware of it.

This is problematic for the work we wish to do here. This is because whenever you react in this way, you form an energetic link with the object or situation with which you are unhappy, resulting in you attracting more of those sorts of unwanted interactions. Think of it as a kind of spider's web you throw out to the person or situation you dislike; your thoughts mean that you are tied until you cut the strands of that web.

The best way to weaken those ties is to recognize straight away the moment you are entering into this scenario. Immediately and consciously think up a reason borne out of compassion for the person who has upset you. 'Perhaps this person is in a huge rush or has troubles in their life that make them insensible to what they're doing. Perhaps they have been treated discourteously all their lives and only know how to behave discourteously as a result. I bless them on their path and wish them a better journey ahead.' Smile as you extend this blessing and it will enrich you as well as the person you are having good thoughts about. The Hawaiian shamanic practitioner, Serge Kahili King, said in a workshop once that when you criticize anything, you create a layer of tension that has an effect on your mind and tenses your body. As such, say true things about what you like rather than talk about what you dislike.

This regular change in your default thoughts will prevent negative cords forming, but you can also dissolve or cut them through your own energy clearing.

CORD CUTTING

It is not just negative cords that are linked to us; each and every interaction creates a cord. Our strongest cord is the link to our biological mother. Even if you never knew your mother, if your mother was abusive or she has died, the link remains a primary one. This is not because of who your human mother is; it is because this is the birth cord — the interaction that made you manifest from divine energy, it is representative of the divine 'mother', the source of all creation. When we speak of cord cutting, you cannot sever this cord, but you can certainly sever any negative ones that are connecting you to your human mother.

Just before you take any of the baths in the following section, stand naked in front of a mirror. If you don't have a mirror somewhere you are able to stand naked, or you don't have a mirror large enough, don't worry. Just stand up straight with nothing around you and your feet firmly planted on the floor.

1. Half close your eyes until your vision is slightly blurred.

2. Using your right hand, take the flat of your hand and pass it over your body, starting at the crown and slowly going over each part of your body. Don't touch your skin; just pass your hand close to your body as if you are stroking your protective sheath.

3. Try and feel where the energy feels 'sticky' or otherwise denser. You may you feel this at your throat; this is very common for people who don't know what to say when they are being verbally attacked, and can only come up with an appropriate response once the moment has passed.

4. When you get to such a place, scoop the energy up with your hand and throw it away from your body. This is just what you would do if you walked into a cobweb and were removing it from your body. You may even 'feel' strands like hairs when you are doing this.

5. When you have done this, immediately have one of the baths described on the following pages.

RITUAL BATHING

Bathing has been proven to be wonderful for the circulation, and due to the changes in your body temperature when you emerge from a hot bath, this will help you have a good night's sleep. The Japanese have a bath ritual called *ofuro*, which often takes place collectively at a public bathhouse called an *onsen*. The Romans also elevated bathing to a ritual art, building beautiful aqueducts near healing springs to enable bathers to take the waters.

Santeria, the Caribbean tradition that developed from the West African Yoruba religion in Cuba, also relies heavily on a ritual bathing practice. Santeria is a Spanish word that means 'worship of the saints', and was developed to hide the worship of Orishas (Yoruba deities and human embodiments of the spirits) behind Western saints in the Roman Catholic religion. Important within the tradition is the connection with the Egun (ancestors).

Overleaf are a couple of baths that help with clearing your personal energy and appealing to your Egun for help and guidance.

Energetic Hygiene

The queen's bath

This is a bath primarily for women, particularly those suffering from a lack of self-esteem or who regularly find themselves in unhappy circumstances, such as bad relationships or difficult living situations.

Ingredients

GOAT'S MILK
1 cup

FLOWER PETALS
White or yellow gold
– avoid roses as their special energy is not
compatible with the baths described here

FLORIDA WATER
Available online or in any store selling
Caribbean or Latin American products –
use the amount that feels right to you

HONEY

2 WHOLE COCONUTS

Instructions

1. Run a hot bath.

2. Pour the goat's milk, petals, Florida water and the water from one of the coconuts (I keep a hammer for cracking open coconuts – it is more potent than just buying coconut water as its energy is contained in the nut), into the bath. Do this with intent, knowing that you are asking your ancestors to bless the water that you are about to get into.

3. Crack open the second coconut and, standing on a towel, pour the water over your head.

4. Take the honey and rub it all over your body, concentrating on the belly and navel.

5. Get into the bath and soak, imagining that all psychic 'dirt' is coming away in the water and all the good energy of the honey, flowers and perfumed water is entering your body.

6. Afterwards you can shower as normal.

7. Thank your ancestors before you go to sleep that night.

Luck bath

This is suitable for both men and women and it removes bad luck as well as strengthening your power. Have this bath early on a day when having flowers and leaves dried on you will not matter as you will not wash or brush off any remnants of this bath until the next day.

Ingredients

BASIL
A bunch, finely chopped

PARSLEY
A bunch, finely chopped

PETALS
from a bunch of flowers (avoid roses, see page 36)

FLORIDA WATER
see page 36

WHISKY
A small bottle

TOBACCO
A pinch

Instructions

1. Mix all the ingredients in a bowl and leave overnight covered with a white muslin cloth.

2. In the morning, run a hot bath and, sitting in that bath, ritually pour the bowl of bath ingredients over your head. It will feel cold, but you should feel fine about it since you are sat in a hot bath. Do not submerge your head and resist the urge to wipe away any leaves left stuck to you.

3. Sit in the bath with your eyes shut for a while thinking about what you would like to manifest in your life and the ways in which you seek protection from the spirits and your ancestors. If your belief system does not allow for spirits, deities or ancestor guides, you can express gratitude to the secular universal energy that comprises us and all things. You should leave the flowers and leaves to dry on you naturally, only washing them off the next morning.

Tips

- Placing a strainer in your bath drain will prevent leaves and flower petals blocking your pipes.

- Despite the sacred and ritual nature of these baths, you can put any waste leaves and petals in your compost or usual disposal.

Energetic Hygiene

Creating some

S P A C E

for energy work

Your home is where you will create your charms and it needs to be able to support energy work. This means that you should have a clear, calm space. It goes without saying that clutter is not helpful when it comes to energy work; this is not because it isn't pretty to look at, but because of the guilt you feel when you look at something you have yet to deal with.

Clutter is essentially decisions you aren't making, so the first thing you have to do is trust yourself to make decisions regarding your possessions. This will support your trust in your own abilities to create the life you want.

DECLUTTER

- Don't handle anything more than once and don't put it down until you have decided precisely what to do with it — find it a home, put it in a bag to go to the charity shop or throw it away if it is broken.

- Don't get waylaid with 'I might need this' or 'I could fix this' — you could, but you haven't. So either fix it immediately or put it in an appropriate place and diarize exactly when you'll have the time and tools to fix it. Otherwise, discard.

- Don't throw out things that don't belong to you, but do ask those who live with you if their property has a home. If not, make a home for it, if they don't want to get rid of it. Having a place to put something that is always getting in your way will stop you resenting it — and the person it belongs to!

CLEAN

- Once you are rid of the clutter, clean your room from top to bottom. Get help if you can't manage it yourself or even hire a professional to do a one-off clean if you can afford it.

- Use ecologically sound cleaning materials as you want to ensure that you are keeping the planet as healthy as you want your home to be. A lot of traditional cleaning solutions, such as lemon juice and vinegar, are natural and only require elbow grease.

- Don't forget the bits that you can't see such as behind picture frames and cobwebs in corners. Get a ladder for the parts of the room you can't reach and carefully get rid of all dirt, seen and unseen. It will change the feeling in the room.

Energetic Hygiene

CHARGE YOUR ROOM

You may then look around at your tidy and clean room and think your work is done: it isn't. Everything is energetically charged as well. Cleaning and tidying start to shift the energetic dust, but it doesn't clean it up, so you can have a perfectly clean and tidy space that is energetically filthy, because it is or has been the scene of trauma or of repressed rage and negative emotion. There are several ways you can clear a space energetically.

For example, you can:

- Smudge a room by passing appropriate burning herbs or spices through it — sage is traditionally used for this purpose, but you can also use rosemary, basil or cloves.

- Scatter sea salt over the carpet ensuring that you go into the corners, leaving it for an hour or two, and then vacuuming it up.

- Place a bowl of filtered water in each corner of the room, blow into each bowl while holding the intent to energetically clear the room into the water; leave for an hour and then pour the water away on your lawn, or into a drain or running water.

- You can also clear a room with sound, using either chanting, drumming or even a handclap in each corner of the room, as long as you visualize the sound waves cleaning out the room's energy.

Energetic rituals

You should feel a shift in your energy and the energy of the room that you practiSe in when you have finished the clearing as per the instructions above, irrespective of which methods you use. However, it important to maintain that feeling in order for your charms to be effective. Here are some rituals and routines that will help you.

MORNING

This daily morning bathing ritual will keep your energy up all day long and help you on days where things aren't quite right.

- **CLEANSING** = While you are washing your face and brushing your teeth, take water in your right palm and touch it three times to the top of your head, each time saying, 'May divinity flow through me today.'

- **SEEING CLEARLY** = Then do the same at the point of your third eye, between your eyebrows, saying three times, 'May I see clearly today.'

- **SPEAKING WELL** = Then at your throat, again three times, saying at each splash, 'May I speak well of all today.'

- **LOVE FLOW** = In the shower, take water in your right hand and hold it over your chest, saying, 'May love flow through me today.' Do not splash at this lower energy centre as the energy here is of a different movement.

- **PROTECTION** = At your belly button, take water into your right hand and holding it there say, 'May the Divine protect me today and always.'

- **LOVE OVER FEAR** = At the point halfway between your belly button and your genitals, take water in your right hand and hold it there saying, 'May I choose love over fear.'

- **FINDING STRENGTH** = Finally, wash at the point of your perineum (between your genitals and your anus), saying, 'May I be rooted in the strength and power of my ancestors and spirit guides.'

Energetic Hygiene

EVENING

This simple evening routine will help ground you in your home and make it a haven for you. If you have time and want to do so, you can also have a specific time (perhaps half an hour before bed) where you lower the lights, light some perfumed candles or incense and change into more comfortable clothes. Having a routine for relaxing at home is a great boon for energy work as it will ensure you have a place of sanctuary.

- **TIDY UP** = Have a 15-minute tidy up of your house when you get home from work. Your instinct will be to sit and relax on the sofa as soon as you get in, but while the kettle is boiling or the wine is breathing, have a very quick whizz around and ensure everything is back where it should be.

- **ENERGY TUNE UP** = Tune into the energy of your home at the end of the day — does anywhere feel particularly disturbed? Do you feel cold in a spot of your house? Or have any sense of general unease in a particular room? Smudge (see page 42) it to ensure that the energy stays clear and keep an eye on it over the coming days.

- **GRATITUDE BLESSING** = Before you go to bed, thank your body for sustaining you throughout the day. We can have a lot of negative self-talk about our bodies, but they are miraculous vehicles to which we should be very grateful. In bed, do the same for your house. A roof over your head is a blessing many don't enjoy, so express gratitude to the home that holds you each night.

WEEKLY

These weekly routines will ensure that your home remains a place that inspires you, supports you and attracts the highest good to you and your loved ones. If you can get everyone involved, all the better.

- **HOUSE BLESSING** = Once a week, you should do a house blessing through the medium of sweeping. Using a besom or natural broom, sweep your floors, moving everything towards the door out of each room, and eventually sweep the dust and dirt over your threshold, out of the front or back door. You can sweep it up once it is past your threshold. Then do the practical step of vacuuming. Your intentional sweeping will have disturbed any stagnant energy and the vacuuming is simply to physically clean the space.

- **WEEKLY CLEAN** = When this is done, wash out a clean, lint-free cloth, and put a couple of drops of essential oils on it (use the one that appeals to you the most or choose from the correspondences on page 49).

You can find many different oil blends out there – speak to an aromatherapist and see if they can create a blend that works best for you on all levels. Wipe all your skirting boards and surfaces that can be touched with oil. As you go, imagine a golden sheen is appearing on those surfaces and sealing them.

- **WATER PLANTS** = Water your plants as necessary, having a little chat with them if you're so inclined. This is also the time to remove any dead leaves or do any trimming if the season is right.

- **MAKE A BREW** = Finally, after your weekly clean is over (and bear in mind the routines above are in addition to whatever your usual cleaning regime is), brew a cup of tea.

Energetic Hygiene

MONTHLY

PARTY TIME = Once a month, hold a party to honour the energies that help you and elevate your energy to a higher plane. There is no point doing all this energy work to protect yourself when there is no joy in having done it or no reminding yourself of what the whole point of living is. So, once a month, throw a party — even if it is just for yourself.

Now, when we think of parties, we think of the expense and invites and loud music and overall organizational hassle. This is not what I mean here. You are changing the energy of your home by inviting others into it; that can be for a very sedate and sophisticated tea party with only two other friends, or it can be an elaborate masked ball. It can even be a night that you put aside to celebrate with your spirits and ancestors alone with good food and drink and a movie that reminds you of the world beyond the mundane. The important thing is the feeling that the night gives you. The anticipation beforehand, the joy of the actual night, and the feeling of satisfaction you get afterwards as you clean up and remember everything that happened during the evening.

GOING OUT = If you are unable to entertain at home, it also fine to go out and see others, as you carry your energy with you all the time, and you will bring back that elevated feeling when you return. You could arrange to meet at a new bar or restaurant. If you do, pay attention to the whole night, from what people are wearing to the décor of the place, to the drinks consumed. Turn up with all your attention and keep your mobile phone tucked away in your bag so that you engage directly and openly with your friends in real life.

LISTENING TO YOUR INTUITION

Just remember though, if your intuition tells you not to go out —
because you're coming down with an illness or you're not up for
company that night — there is no shame in cancelling or rescheduling.
True friends understand when we're not able to meet a commitment.

However, if this happens to you a lot, in your next meditation do
think about why this might be. Ask your ancestors, guides or
subconscious to reveal why you often feel the need to cancel. Are
you afraid of something? Are you even afraid of having a good time
and leaving your unhappiness behind? Sometimes people are so afraid
that everyone will think they are okay and stop checking in on them if
they are strong, healthy and happy that they retain a vulnerability
they could easily lose. Reliability is a good trait to have and if you are
finding yourself becoming more unreliable, have a proper conversation
with yourself — without judgement or beating yourself up about it — to
discover why that might be.

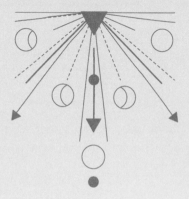

MONTHLY ENERGY TEST

As part of your regular routine, take a day each month to perform an energy test in your home to ensure that all is well.

1. Ensure you are not hungry, ill or otherwise unmotivated when beginning. Try and pick the same date each month to perform this test.

2. Take off your shoes and socks and make sure your feet are flat on the floor of your home.

3. Starting at your front door, walk each room (including your hallway and any cupboards) with your hands in front of you open-palmed.

4. 'Feel' the energy in each part of your home. Pass your hand into corners and really try and sense how that area feels. Some parts of your home may feel more stagnant than others. Some will feel colder and others will feel wonderful.

5. When you find an area that feels less than wonderful, take a look for any physical reason first. Is there clutter here? An heirloom that always makes you feel guilty for not loving it? Perhaps it is just dusty and dirty? Address the physical issues first — declutter, give the heirloom to a family member who will love it or put it into storage where you won't see it — then make the area squeaky-clean.

6. If it looks physically okay, use one of the techniques on page 42 to clear the energy of the place.

7. Finally, go out for a walk and return at least half an hour later and do your barefoot walk again to see if the energy has shifted in the area that concerned you.

ESSENTIAL OIL CORRESPONDENCES

BASIL
to enhance wealth

BERGAMOT
to stimulate energy

JASMINE
to cure insomnia,
remember happy memories

ORANGE
also good for physical
energy and cheerfulness

EUCALYPTUS
releases negative
energy from fights

LAVENDER
aids good sleep and encourages
good-naturedness

CLARY SAGE
destresses and helps acceptance

YLANG YLANG
promotes romantic love and
enhances sexuality

State
of being

In our ancient societies, we knew that there was more to the world than what met the eye. We had a much more friendly relationship with gods, spirits and dead ancestors. We even had a much more friendly relationship with fear. We knew that fear was necessary on occasion to motivate us; it was the companion to our rites of passage, the bedfellow to our big life milestones. We knew fear to be natural and, pardon the paradox, that it was nothing to be afraid of. Now, we avoid it at all costs.

When you begin energy work, there will be miracles and coincidences that will leave you in shock and awe. Sudden windfalls of money that are precisely what you asked for down to the last penny. A strange connection between two parts of your life you were never aware of that suddenly brings you the opportunity you had been praying for. And, on occasion, a glimpse into parallel worlds and spirit worlds. If you are interested in understanding the true nature of the magickal being that you are, by your very birthright, you have to get used to that sort of thing.

Energetic Hygiene

YOUR ALTAR

In order to communicate with your ancestors and/or spirit guides you can set up an altar (see also page 133).

- Consecrate any flat plane, keep it clean and place sacred objects upon it.

- Sit or stand or kneel before it and, through the very act of being there, enter into a state of calm meditation.

- Place on the altar the charms that you will learn about in the next section, or you can keep it clear of anything except a single flame that you light whenever you want to enter into that state of communion.

- Some people will have an icon or image that reminds them of the deity that they worship.

- If you have a spare bedroom where you can set up an altar, so much the better. Keep this room for your energy work, such as meditation and crafting charms.

- Bedrooms are good for this purpose as it should be a space that brings you a sense of rest and relaxation.

- Keep electrical devices out of this room so that you enter a state of focus when you go in there.

- If you don't have a spare room, a corner of any of your rooms can be used; just don't put the altar in a high traffic area where you will constantly be disturbed.

HOW TO COMMUNICATE WITH THE SPIRITS

Energetic Hygiene

Once you have set up your altar, light the candle and sit or stand before it for a while, steadying your breathing and letting your focus in your vision soften.

1. Begin by saying, 'For the highest good, and with the help of my ancestral spirits, I petition the universal energy to answer my question.'

2. Then, pick a single question on which you need guidance and hold the question in your mind. Phrase it in such a way that it will help you decide on whether an outcome is right for you, rather than whether or not it will happen. For example, if you are worried about the state of your relationship, rather than asking, 'Will my partner leave me?', instead ask, 'Are we right for each other?'

3. Pay attention to any images, words or ideas that pop into your head when you're asking in the intentional way. They are all clues as to what your spirits are telling you.

4. Don't keep asking the same question. There is nothing more annoying for those giving advice than to be asked the same thing over and over in the hope of getting a different answer. It may give you an idea of what YOU'd like to happen, but that isn't the same as what the spirits or your highest destiny has in mind for you.

NOURISHING YOUR BODY

A really important part of energy work is what you put into your body. When you undertake shamanic work, you often fast beforehand in order to purify the body and enable better communion with spirits. In protection work, the denser the body, the better. This is because you are closing down your body to anyone or anything other than the ancestral or divine spirits that you yourself are inviting in for connection and guidance.

I tend to find that people truly love this part of my advice. You should eat what makes you happy. Obviously not to excess, because that might cause you other physical problems, but it should be what makes your toes curl with pleasure. Once you have properly honoured and connected with your own energy, you will find that you know precisely what you need to feel good. Sometimes your body will crave salt because it needs it. At other times, this might be sweet things or vegetables or meat. Listen to its needs and don't follow faddy diets. Eat less of whatever you are craving if you are concerned that it will cause you to put on unwanted weight, but don't deny yourself due to any dietary regime.

You will find that historically a number of occultists were traditionally larger than average. This is because the density of the body aids in providing another layer of energy before anything intrusive can breach the protective sheath or reach the naf.

In South America, shamans work with 'teacher plants' such as ayahuasca, peyote and San Pedro. It is believed that these plants are governed by spirits who can give you healing information if you commune with them. I have worked with such teacher plants before and, in authentic ceremonies, you must follow a very bland diet in the weeks running up to the ceremony. Meat, salt and spices are often stopped and you fast on the day of the ceremony. This is in order to make your body a comfortable place for the plant spirit to inhabit and commune with.

Such spiritual work requires you to make your body lighter and more open to the spirits. However, in protection magick, you often have to ground yourself to protect yourself from the spirit world. It is grounding to eat meat, spices and salt.

Ethically our farming systems are indefensible, but more and more higher welfare meat is available in our stores and you should choose that, even if it is more expensive. Eat less, but eat more ethically. If you're a vegan, choose mushrooms and potatoes as foods to ground yourself. If you can bake, make your own bread — this is a very good way to nourish yourself and your family. Think about the safety, health and happiness of you and your loved ones while you knead the bread, and you will produce a loaf that is not just a foodstuff but is a magickal spell of protection for everyone who eats it.

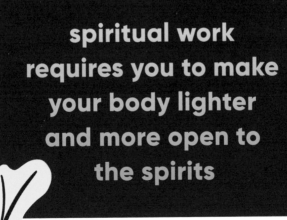

spiritual work requires you to make your body lighter and more open to the spirits

Everyday comfort

You know that feeling you get when you get into a bed made with fresh linen after bathing, the scent of a night-time essential oil blend is in the room, and all is calm and peaceful? This section will help you achieve that 'aah' level of comfort.

Why is this important? It is because if you embrace everyday comfort, anything that is energetically or physically uncomfortable will become glaringly obvious. You will recognize it far more easily if you've become accustomed to everyday comfort. Not only that, but it is a good way to live and honour your corporeal existence.

TEXTURES

- Buy some soft socks or cloth slippers that you can put on when you get in to get cosy.

- Find a warm throw for your sofa so you always have something to put over you when you're snuggling down with a good book.

- Eat foods that you find comforting — it may be the texture of a certain cheese or baked item that makes it taste especially good.

- Iron your clothes — it sounds like a bit of a pedantry but ironed clothes feel better against the skin, making them an everyday comfort for you.

SENSES

- Find the tea blend that makes you feel most comforted — it is Earl Grey for me — and always have it to hand.

- Have a signature scent for your home — this will be a combination of your cleaning materials, some incense or scented candles and your own unique scent.

- Don't wear anything that makes you uncomfortable — it will make you grumpy.

- Listen to soothing music when in the bath to add to the atmosphere.

LETTING ENERGY FLOW

I once house-sat for a friend whose home was the most infuriating place I have ever stayed in. If you went to get something out of a drawer, the drawer fell apart or got stuck. There were odd, heavy bits of furniture blocking your path, meaning that you always stubbed a toe or banged a shin when walking past. His kitchen had a broken window covered with a piece of cardboard. His plumbing also left much to be desired. I was very confused as my friend had both the money and sense to take care of all these things. He said he had tried to book appointments to get these problems fixed but no one had turned up. That just didn't seem credible to me, so I made some calls while he was away.

On the first day his assessment was correct — people either didn't answer or didn't turn up when they said they would. So then, knowing what I do about energy, I mended the worst of his drawers. The carpenter called me back that afternoon and arranged to come and do the other small fixes in the house. Next I tided away the loose glass from the window, removed the cardboard and called the glazing company again. I got through immediately and a very helpful man came to replace the glass an hour later. Then the plumber arrived unprompted with huge apologies for not having come earlier. In the space of two days, the main fixes were done. Then — with my friend's permission — I re-arranged his furniture and made the energy flow better in his house. The whole feel of the place immediately changed and it was no longer a house at war with its occupant. Once you begin to commit to ensuring that energy can flow freely, things start to run much more smoothly.

What happened in the example above is that I committed to fixing the things that were wrong and the Universe conspired to help me. When you make a decision to get your energetic house in order, the Universe or Divine energy or luck will be on your side. However, you must make that commitment first, and one of the easiest and most enjoyable ways you can do that is to keep an eye open for your comfort at all times.

Treat yourself like a most beloved friend who is staying with you. It is your job, as a good host, to make sure your pal is comfortable at all times and enjoys her stay. Ask yourself the questions opposite.

I committed to fixing the things that were wrong and the Universe conspired to help me

THE FRIEND TEST

Everyday comfort involves treating yourself well, and if this takes you thinking about how you would treat others that you respect in order to treat yourself the same way, then use that as a prop to get yourself in the right mindset.

- What would you do if your friend was wearing ill-fitting shoes or uncomfortable clothes? Would you offer her insoles, suggest she buy new shoes, let her change into something comfortable from your own wardrobe?

- If your pal was coming round, would you be happy with her seeing your house as it is right now? Is it clean? Is it comfortable?

- What sort of food and drink would you serve her? Would you serve it on a nice dish or out of the carton?

- Would you force her to watch/do whatever it was that the most vocal member of the family wanted to see and do? Or would you give her a choice and let her decide what she most wanted to do with her time?

Energetic Hygiene

Energy flow

Once you're in the mindset of creating everyday comfort
for yourself, you can also go through your house and
detect places of stuck energy or tension. The way to do
this is to notice when you're next frustrated by some
element of your living space.

Bath Bliss

Do you huff when you realize
that you have to go back to your
bedroom to get the nice bath salts
because you forgot to take them in
with you? Find a place either in or
near the bathroom where you
can keep the salts.

Laundry Life-hack

Is your laundry basket hidden
away so that none of your family can
be bothered to put their dirty clothes
in it? Buy a prettier basket (or
several) and keep it somewhere
your family can drop their
clothes in on their way
past.

Toys Tidied

Do you keep stepping on your
children's toys? Colourful bins
around the edge of a room
where small hands can
place their toys with
ease will help.

Key Magic

Can you never find your keys? A set of hooks by the front door or a plate in the hallway where you can always hang or drop your keys when you come in will work wonders.

Take the Lead

Is it someone else's 'stuff' that is getting in your way? Tidy your own things away first and keep them tidy for a while and you'll soon notice that your arch-ne-mess-is (see what I did there?) also starts putting his or her stuff away too.

Table Troubles

Is your coffee table too large and unwieldy? Sell it and use the money to buy another one more in proportion with your requirements.

Energetic Hygiene

This is an ongoing investigation, so do keep detecting where things can be better utilized. You will find that as you begin the process of making energy flow better in your home, you will suddenly get brilliant ideas for where things can go that will work better.

Once you get to the stage that the energy is flowing well through your home, and you are also comfortable in your body and what you're wearing, you can begin the process of creating protection charms. You have laid the important foundations on which you can build your magickal symbols of security and prosperity.

Charms

and Symbols

Our earliest examples of art show that even then we had the ability to make symbols that represented our desired outcomes. We understood and believed in sympathetic magick: our ancestors drew pictures of successful hunts before going out on real hunts in anticipation that their symbolic etchings might come to pass. They drew vaginas and phalluses hoping for fertility and children borne of that fecundity. Humans have carried trinkets in their pockets to ward off ill luck for millennia and believed that there is a kingdom of spirits out there to guard us and all that was needed was to determine the correct way to contact them.

Power of charms

As the Abrahamic religions took over from paganism and animism, our belief in the power of charms and amulets did not fall way – in fact, it was taken up by these new religions and incorporated into them. So there is the Jewish mezuzah (a charm that uses prayers placed into a container and hung on the wall or around the neck); Christian verbal charms (particularly prevalent in Ireland where sickness was kept at bay by invoking a particular saint in a specific way that was quite different from devotionals or other accepted prayers); and Muslim amulets (in which magick squares are made corresponding to Quranic verse numbers and inserted into a square metal locket to be worn around the neck). Making ancient protection charms acceptable to monotheistic religions was done by taking old practices and attributing their workings to the Judeo-Christian-Islamic God.

While our ancestors sought to avoid disease and pestilence with their charms – and in many cases, ever-prevalent early death – we can use the same principles to concentrate our minds on manifesting the things that cause us to feel happier and more secure. We are now lucky enough to have excellent doctors and so no longer need charms to bring about healing. However, today we do have a great deal of mental distress with the level of confrontation that exists as part of normal life. It is certainly possible to focus the mind on objects that give us comfort and protection from these conflicts.

LISTENING TO YOUR INTUITION

While verbal charms formed an important part of historic magickal protection, it is far more difficult to use them in everyday life. This is because you're likely to get strange looks if you start incantations on your average train carriage. However, the potency of charms that are created at a time of relaxed intent at home and then carried with you, either as a piece of jewellery or as a pocket token, is just as good.

Written charms are also potent, although their complexity varies wildly from simple symbols to the somewhat more difficult knowledge found in esoteric books. The words within those books would not necessarily be invoked but the number of the passage within them would be written on a slip of paper in a diagram that had the same effect as the verse or passage itself.

John Dee and Edward Kelley, in the late 16th century, wrote a book that was, they claimed, dictated to them by angels. It was in a language that has since been dubbed Enochian, in the light of Enoch being the last man who is said to have spoken this divine tongue. Since that time, occultists have formulated magick based on this Enochian language and the letters associated with it. This complex system is very much akin to a number of Arabic occult practices and is worth looking into once you are ready for a more advanced look at charms, spells and divination.

Dee and Kelley's writings are, however, an example of how charms are traditionally said to work. They usually rely on a deity or entities that the charm-maker appeals to in order to get the work done. In our modern age, we rarely give such agency to supernatural forces, preferring to rely on ourselves. However, just because we have chosen to ignore the gods and other generally invisible beings, this doesn't mean they have abandoned us. To be called upon to work with an entity is a wonderful outcome that can happen to any one of us, if only we have the eyes and ears to recognize the call when it comes.

Charms and Symbols

ASKING FOR HELP

Here are some ways in which you can 'tune in' to see if there is a spirit guide or entity that would like to work with you:

- Keep an eye out for any image or glyph that you regularly notice in a variety of different places. For example, are you seeing the sign for women more often and not just on toilet doors (meaning the astrological sign for Venus rather than the outline of a figure wearing a skirt)? This could indicate that you should work with the goddess Venus in all her myriad forms throughout the world.

- Pay close attention to your dreams, for this is where we are often approached by entities that can only communicate with our unconscious minds. If you have a dream that is so powerful it stays with you, write it down and then look up any associations with what you dreamt. At the age of seven I had a dream that meant I was being called by the goddess Kali and her energetic equivalent goddess Sekhmet, but I only realized the true meaning many years later.

- Have you heard an unusual word from a number of different sources on numerous occasions? Look up the etymology, or history, of that word. Learn where it came from and if there are any associations that resonate with you. It may not have anything to do with the meaning of the word. For example, while it means to take offence, I noticed the word 'umbrage' appearing more and more in my daily life. The root of the word comes from 'shade' or 'shadow', and even used to mean the lovely dappled shade created by the leaves of a mature tree. I took this to mean that my greatest achievements lay in the dark or 'shade', and so I developed my interest in the hidden arts of the occult.

- Finally, you can also use bibliomancy to help you. This is the practice of taking a book, opening it at random and reading a line that catches your eye. This will be a message from any entity that wants to work with you and your protective charms.

Charms and Symbols

Verbal charms

Charms can be verbal — working sounds and/or words — or physical, using text or objects. They can also include elements of both.

Sound is an important component in working with charms. Many charms just involved the spoken word and we can find these worldwide. For example, in the 17th and 18th centuries, Russians were using many verbal charms (*zagovory*) in order to affect the outcome of court cases and influence the Tsar and the royal family. Researcher Andrei L. Toporkov writes: 'The magical purpose of these verbal charms was to have an influence on authorities and judges, to alter the way they felt and their will, their mood and spiritual condition.

The tradition of incantations if seen as a whole did not force a person to take this or that specific attitude towards the authorities, but rather offered the possibility of choice either to consider the object of the charm as an implacable foe, deserving of annihilation (if only symbolic), or as someone more positive, from whom love is coaxed.'

These verbal charms were ritualistically incanted before the inciting incident such as a court case. Here is an example:

> Give to me, slave of God, the heart of a ferocious lion-beast and a larynx like the jaw of the prowling wolf. Let my opponent, my ruler [insert name], have the heart of a hare, ears of a grouse and eyes like a dead man's corpse; that he not manage to open his mouth and that his clear eyes be troubled, that he not rail against me in his zealous heart, that his white hands not be raised up against me, servant of God [insert name].

The aim was to cause the person in charge to become enchanted and unable to make any decisions against the person casting the charm. A lot of spellwork worldwide has these stated aims, to affect outcomes where the petitioner is powerless but may regain their power through magickal means. It is the basis of a lot of modern binding spellwork by witches who wish to stop others doing harm. However, it can also be used to avoid justice.

Physical charms

Here we will focus on textual and physical charms rather than verbal ones. However, you can imbue them with more power by chanting over them after you have finished making them (or receiving them if made by someone else). You can also add things to them, such as shells, wooden chips and metal coins, that make them jangle or make a noise when you move or the air moves through them. Archaeologists have found babies' rattles painted with angry faces and surmised that they may have been used for more than just keeping the infant entertained. It was thought that a jangling noise frightened away evil spirits.

While sound is traditionally the best charm that can be used, in the modern world textual charms are easier to make and use.

A textual charm is written on a piece of paper and either ingested by swallowing with water, or folded up very small and put into an amulet necklace and worn at all times.

An interesting form of a textual charm are the incantation bowls of Babylon in the 4th-6th centuries, utilizing the Jewish occult to protect against Lilith, a demoness believed to kill children. In the centre of the bowl would be a figure depicting Lilith and in circular writing around it would be incantations against her. The bowl would then be buried upside down under the structure of the house or in its grounds to 'trap' Lilith beneath it.

AMULETS

Amulets inscribed with the names of three angels — Senoy, Sansenoy and Semangelof (occasionally these are a different set of angels and the archangel Michael also features regularly) — were put around the necks of newborn boys to protect them from Lilith who had made a deal with those angels to leave alone any child bearing their mark.

In ancient Rome, freeborn boys were given a *bulla* (amulet) nine days after birth, which would protect the child from evil spirits, and was only removed when the boy came of age. Girls were given another sort of amulet called a *lunula*, which was worn until the day before her marriage when it was removed along with all the other trappings of childhood. These are surprisingly similar in shape and appearance to the *tawiz* you see in the Indian sub-continent.

The 4th-century collection of Greek books called the *Kyranides* gives lists of the type of magical amulets one might use to protect against demons of different orders. For example, a rather unsavoury amulet was to carry the eyeballs of a hyena in a purple pouch. This was said to guard against the Gello, a demon known to suffocate infants and cause stillbirths.

While our modern sensibilities mean we are no longer as concerned by demons and evil spirits, we do still worry about naturally occurring troubles that often just seem down to simple bad luck. It can help to have divine energies on side to mitigate against the effect of such misfortune.

Some helpful energies you can attract before beginning your work with the charms are those of the celestial bodies. This meditation is taken from the Sufi practices of my family and was given to me by my father. It will certainly help clear your energy before magickal work but, if you find yourself impatient to get going with creating your personal charm, you can do the cleansing visualization on page 20 instead as a shortened version of this.

some helpful energies you can attract before beginning your work with the charms are those of the celestial bodies

Star alignment

There is an ancient belief that everything in Heaven and Earth is connected and influences each other. The Sufis call this 'Unity of Being' (*wahdat al wujud*). This star alignment meditation is based on this principle. It is a way of using the positive energies of stars to dissolve any limitations or negative influences in your life. You can improve your experience of life here on Earth through a readjustment and revitalization of your natal horoscope on a spiritual plane and ready yourself for magickal work.

Beginners don't need to know the ins and outs of the planets they were born under. All the stars have their own particular energies, both positive and negative, which are reflected in a natal chart. For example, Venus's positive energies represent love, friendship, harmony, sympathy, a social life, an artistic nature, etc. However, if Venus is sitting in an uncomfortable place in the birth chart or Venus is afflicted (meaning if other planets are sitting opposite or at right angles to it in the sky at the time of your birth), then it may manifest itself as over-sensitivity, laziness, superficiality, a false self-image, arrogance, indulgence, excessive sexuality, extravagance, etc. Using the meditation that follows, you can learn to turn such negative traits into positive ones. It is a general meditation, but if you would like to work on the planets most useful to you personally, either ask an astrologer to do your chart or visit the astrology website recommended on page 154 to get a free copy of your birth chart. You will need to know the time, date and place of your birth, so start annoying your mother with specific questions.

A meditation

The meditation creates harmony within your energy make-up and makes you a stronger vessel for doing the energy work required in making and using protection charms.

Start the meditation on a Sunday because Sunday is ruled by the Sun, which plays the central role in all meditations on Earth involving the stars and planets. This is a 49-day practice, split into seven-day sections to enable you to take time away from the meditation if you need to. However, you shouldn't stop in the middle of the seven-day cycle as you will have to go back to the beginning of that cycle before you can continue with the meditation. This initial practice is based on seven stars (actually one star, the Sun, five planets and one satellite, the Moon, but let's not quibble).

Begin your practice with the Sun meditation on the opposite page. Follow each step and complete the meditation before going on to the next section.

The next 'star' you'll need to draw down is the Moon. You do the same meditation, this time changing the colour you are imagining to the white of the Moon. When the energies of the Moon are coming down from the crown of your head, imagine that they are flowing into your internal sun. When they mingle, it is not a crash but a relaxed, happy and positive union of colour and energy. When you speak to your internal moon at the end of the meditation, ask that it stay with you for ever and thank it, too. The body of light you have in you now contains sun and moon energies. If during the meditation you feel a tickling sensation or shudders, this is a sign that energies are entering you and you should not be alarmed.

You then go through each of the following stars for seven days each, mixing the colours and energies of each star within your internal ball of light. See pages 76–79 for the colours of the stars and their respective areas of influence.

Instructions

1. Make sure you are sitting comfortably and that you won't be disturbed for at least 30 minutes.

2. Make yourself as relaxed as possible. Ensure your spine is straight, either sitting or lying down, and take 11 deep breaths.

3. Close your eyes. Imagine that at your solar plexus, within your body, there is a space.

4. Once you can visualize that, think about the Sun. Imagine that from your crown all the positive energy, orange light and colour of the Sun is coming down through you to your solar plexus. Increase that energy, really visualize it and gather it up.

5. Once it forms a critical mass, it will become a small sun based at the point of your solar plexus. This internal sun will then provide energy to your entire body.

6. Feel that energy coursing through you. Imagine that the light from this sun is dissolving your internal complexes, inhibitions and worries. The build-up of light and energy should be so great that it begins to come out through your pores and into your aura. Anything dark in your aura is extinguished by this internal light.

7. After this, ask the Sun to stay with you for ever and thank the Sun for being within you.

8. Finish and rise relaxed and full of energy. You need to do this entire process for seven consecutive days. If, in the course of your daily life, you require more energy, imagine a positive vibration from your internal sun giving you power and energy.

Charms and Symbols

The Sun

The Sun governs sunlight and all vital forces that stem from it and flow through the Solar System, allowing life to exist.

COLOUR:
orange

STONES:
diamonds, red garnet

THE SUN SIGNIFIES
power, authority,
pride, ambition, will and desire.

HEALTH:
it rules the heart, circulation,
arteries, eyes, spinal cord
and the vital life force.

The Moon

The Moon signifies mothers and women generally.
Water and liquid are governed by this star, too.

COLOUR:
silvery white

STONES:
moonstone, opals,
milk-white stones

THE MOON GOVERNS
feelings, sensations and
instincts.

HEALTH:
stomach and digestion, bladder,
breasts, womb, child-bearing, the
female cycle, the nervous system.

Mercury

Mercury signifies schools and places of learning.
It governs the intellect and education.

COLOUR:
yellow

STONES:
topaz, agate, marble

MERCURY RULES
thought and reason,
all intellectual faculties
including articulation
and communication.

HEALTH:
the brain and nervous
system, the tongue and
organs of speech, hands.

Venus

Venus signifies beauty, love, luxury,
wealth and pleasure.

COLOUR:
indigo

STONES:
jade, lapis lazuli, beryl

VENUS GOVERNS
the emotions and affections,
particularly romantic love.
Venus also governs good
taste and aesthetics.

HEALTH:
throat, kidneys,
generative system,
indirectly physical beauty.

Charms and Symbols

Mars

Mars signifies war, courage and strength.

COLOUR::
red

STONES::
ruby, bloodstone and red jewels

MARS GOVERNS
strength, courage,
bravery, passion,
self-reliance and anger.

HEALTH::
the external head, the nose and
smell, the reproductive organs,
the gall bladder, fevers, high
temperature, infectious disease,
eruptions, burns, scalds,
bloodshed, sharp pains.

Jupiter

Jupiter signifies wealth, benevolence,
philanthropy and sociability.

COLOUR::
blue and purple

STONES::
turquoise, amethyst

JUPITER GOVERNS
harmony, wealth and
benevolence, good nature
and a love of order.

HEALTH::
feet, thighs, liver, blood,
muscles, growth and digestion.

Saturn

Saturn signifies those aspects that relate
to the earth, including mountains, hills,
caves and even corpses and graves.

COLOUR:
green

STONES:
Sapphire, obsidian, garnet

SATURN GOVERNS
the will and manifests as
self-control, patience,
reserve, austerity, chastity
and practical ability.

HEALTH:
bones, teeth, the spleen,
diseases brought on by cold,
rheumatism, falls, accidents,
depression.

After you have successfully completed the 49 days of this meditation,
you will have an internal solar system (at your solar plexus) to call upon
in times of need. The solar plexus is the seat of your basic self and this
constant source of light and energy will enable you to see any situation
more clearly and will give you the strength to deal with that situation,
resulting in more inner confidence and more control over outer
situations. You can continue to use this as your daily meditation to
concentrate on a specific element in your life; alternatively you can
manifest the energies of all seven stars by imagining the ball radiating
all the stars' colours and energies outward throughout your body,
giving you a rainbow-coloured aura. If you need the energies of a
particular star, concentrate on its colour and you will find that the
energies of the other six stars will help you manifest that particular
energy. Call upon the relevant one when you are working with your
charm of choice.

Charms and Symbols

The chakras
in Sufism

There are usually seven chakras in the Western esoteric system, although the Vedic sources for chakras give a number of different systems with various numbers of chakras. The system I use is the one given within Sufi thought. Here there are six basic chakras:

When creating your personal charm (pages 104–106) you can also use the colours in the chakras opposite to balance anything to do with the associations given, apart from the sixth chakra, which is concerned with death and reunion with the spirit energy from which we all come. There is no point creating a charm against death because it will not work. Our deathday is as certain as our birthday and no amount of charm-making or pleading changes it. You can create a charm for a good death, free of pain and violence, but alas you can't cheat death as we are all mortal beings.

POINT OF MANTLE: situated in the crown of the head.

Colour: a shining, iridescent black

Associations: unity with divine essence and a return to spirit

POINT OF VEILED: situated in the middle of forehead, popularly known as third eye. It is the meeting point between soul (spirit) and the body. Everything from the Divine comes to this point and is then distributed into other points.

Colour: dark blue

Associations: spirituality and otherworldly learning

POINT OF SOUL: its centre is an inch or so below the right breast.

Colour: white

Associations: community, family, ancestors and helping others

POINT OF MYSTERY: situated between the point of heart and soul in the middle of chest.

Colour: green

Associations: learning, adventures and travel

POINT OF HEART: its centre is an inch or so below the left breast.

Colour: orange

Associations: love, relationships and the love of children

POINT OF CARNAL SELF: its centre is in the navel (just below the belly button).

Colour: yellow

Associations: sex, money and status

Charms and Symbols

The seven charms

Beginning with the serpent at the start and end of time, then examining the four elements found in nature, the ubiquitous evil eye defence, and finally, the hamsa, these seven charms will enable you to begin to protect yourself and your home. Each will enable you to bring a different type of protection into your life.

Seven is a potent number and, while there are thousands of charms worldwide for a variety of different problems, these seven are the most universal and easy to use irrespective of where you are in your energetic journey.

On the following pages, we look at charms that can be made from the four classical alchemical elements. These elements originate in ancient Greek philosophy and are good to ground you in the manifest world and protect you from worldly harm.

Charms and Symbols

The
ouroboros

Representing either the Milky Way galaxy or the Sun, the ouroboros (meaning 'the tail-devourer' in Greek) is an ancient symbol found first in the 14th century BCE on a golden shrine in the tomb of the boy king Tutankhamun. Here it is shown twice, an image of the king guarded by an ouroboros at his feet and another at his head. It represents cyclical time and the passage of the year. Birth and death cycles are predicted by the snake or dragon swallowing its own tail because within its death is its renewal.

The symbol then made its way to Greece where it is the oldest known allegorical symbol in alchemy. Here it represented the true nature of things being ultimately one.

It is also found in Norse mythology as the serpent Jörmungandr, who spans the world and holds its tail in its mouth. Quetzalcoatl, the Mesoamerican god, is occasionally also depicted as a looping snake with his tail in his mouth.

This is one of the seven charms because it is a symbol of the true nature of all things. It is a charm that exists all over the world and has a near-universal acceptance as a meaningful commentary on the turning cyclical wheel of our fortunes. Since the dragon or snake of the ouroboros is often shown encircling the Earth, it is also a protective symbol, holding our world within its coils. A spell from a Greek magical papyrus appealing to the Sun god Helios reads: 'Helios is to be engraved on a heliotrope stone as follows: a thick-bodied snake in the shape of a wreath should be having its tail in its mouth. Inside the snake let there be a sacred scarab.'

In Gnostic texts from philosophical and religious movements prominent in the Greco-Roman world in the early Christian era, the ouroboros is also linked to the primordial darkness and, in the *Pistis Sophia* (a manuscript dated around the 3–4th century CE), Jesus says, 'The outer darkness is a great dragon whose tail is in its mouth, and it is outside the whole world, and it surrounds the whole world.'

Often considered the supreme god of the creation, the ouroboros is a great symbol to use in protection magick.

Charms and Symbols

USING THE CHARM

- Spread bird seed in a circle on your bird table on a sunny day, saying to yourself, 'May the protection of Helios be upon me today.'

- Paint it on a stone, as per the instructions on pages 112-113, and carry it as a personal protection charm.

- Make or buy jewellery featuring the motif — my handfasting gift from my husband was a large ouroboros necklace that always makes me feel safer whenever I wear it.

- Print out or draw an ouroboros on a piece of paper and rest your water glass on it daily to ingest its protective spirit by way of magickal contagion.

- If you like tattoos, there are many examples of the symbol used as a protection charm in tattoo form.

- If a permanent tattoo is a step too far, consider making a temporary henna tattoo on your body — especially around the belly button or naf — to see the effect over the days it takes to fade.

OUROBOROS MEDITATION

Some people are scared of snakes and may not want to use the ouroboros as a protective symbol for that reason. If you aren't keen on snakes and serpents, envision the ouroboros energy as coils of light that meet each other rather than the coils of a snake.

1. Sit in a straight-backed chair with your feet flat on the ground and your hands turned palm upwards on your lap.

2. Close your eyes and take three deep breaths in and out through your nose.

3. Imagine that there is a great serpent of light high above your head moving in the infinity symbol, which is a figure of eight on its side.

4. Imagine the snake's head then moving down through the top of your head and through your body's energy centres until it emerges as light under your feet.

5. Then imagine that this light moves upwards in front of you to meet the tail above you. The 'snake' of light then forms a continuous circle with its body within your body.

6. Feel the protective energy of this light and thank it for being with you.

7. When you feel ready, turn your palms downwards, rub your hands on your lap and open your eyes. This ouroboros energy will remain with you as you go about your day.

Charms and Symbols

Air

Air is all around us and is essential to life and yet it is unseen and unconsidered. A charm using this symbol will protect you from all those things associated with air, such as delays with air travel, air pollution, reduced or poor breathing (please don't rely on charms for this and do seek the advice of a health professional). It is also a good protection against anything that has wings, from diseased mosquitoes to anything demonic. The air sign fixes and repels those things that have to use that medium to get at you.

In terms of attraction, when you work with this symbol, you can improve your communication and ability to express yourself. It is the sign of the planet Mercury, which rules over all messages, communications and writing. If you have any legal matters outstanding that you would like to go a particular way, this is the sign to use for a favourable outcome.

USING THE CHARM

- Draw the symbol for air in front of you, imagining it glowing as though you have traced it with a sparkler. Walk through the symbol and go about your day.

- Write a letter to someone you feel can help you in your work and, after writing it, trace the symbol on the letter before you send it. Visualize that person being receptive to you and your letter.

- If you have a tarot pack, take out the ace of swords and place it in front of you while meditating. This will help you focus on the qualities of the air charm and how it can improve your life.

Charms and Symbols

Fire

The Titan Prometheus was punished by the gods for giving people fire - it was considered a gift too valuable for mere mortals. Anyone who has sat in front of a camp fire, enjoying the warmth and the mind-altering feeling, will tell you now magickal this element is. Fire is also a purifier; many spiritual traditions and religions use fire in their ceremonies to sanctify and cleanse the energy of the congregation. Fire is all about action and adventure; it is passionate and untameable. This is an element to use when looking to invigorate your work, and to encourage more risk-taking and less stagnation in your life. If you are using this charm for home protection, ensure you keep it enclosed in a square to represent the hearth, so that the fire is one that is deliberate and helpful.

You can use the ace of wands in meditation if you would like to use a tarot pack to connect with the energy of this charm.

USING THE CHARM

- Draw the fire symbol on some paper, hold the paper in your palm as you say the wish you would like to come true, blow on the paper three times and then burn it in a flame-proof bowl set aside for ritual purposes. Discard the ashes outside, ideally in a wild place.

- Make yourself a hot chocolate with a pinch of chilli flakes in it and use a stick to draw the triangle of the fire symbol in the cream on top. Drink this while thinking about fire's protection in your body and at your heart.

- Whenever you need more energy, wrap your water bottle in a piece of paper with this symbol on it and your water will become charged with energy, putting 'fire' in your belly.

Charms and Symbols

Earth

We are created from clay or earth and, as our bodies decay after death, we return to become the earth again. This element is the stuff that we are made of and is the one most aligned with the practical and the real. However, this is not to say that there is nothing spiritual in it. It is the earthy green of nature, the smell after rain on parched ground, the joy you have in eating a cream bun. It is the pleasures your flesh affords you. It has associations with money, prosperity and carnal gratification. This charm is the one to use if you are beset with worries about your material well-being. It is one that works best when accompanied by practical action as well as the spiritual act of making and working with a charm. So, as well as painting this symbol on your money box, you should call a debt charity if you're struggling with your finances. In addition to drawing it at the top of your shopping list, you should cut out coupons or contact a food bank if you feel you will need it. This charm is magickal but also wants you to work toward your own salvation. The ace of pentacles is the tarot card you need for meditation on this element.

USING THE CHARM

- Keep this symbol on a slip of paper in your wallet.

- Create a fridge magnet featuring the symbol and stick it on your fridge to encourage abundance in food and drink.

- When growing your own food, put this symbol on a wooden plant marker and stick it in the ground or pot where you are hoping for crops.

Charms and Symbols

Water

Do you believe in mermaids? I do! This is the element that will enable you to communicate with them, and with the powerful sea goddess, Mami Wata. If you're journeying over the seas, you will need her patronage. This element governs the emotions and inner states. You will need the help of this charm if you are having relationship problems or finding it hard to deal with emotions such as anger or sadness. These emotions are an important part of being human, so the aim is not to stop feeling them; it is more about managing them in a way that is appropriate and helps you to heal. Water is one of the greatest healers we have: from the ineffable perfection of a hot bath in winter, to the restorative drink at the end of a long run, our survival and happiness depend on our access to clean, safe water. Remember to be cautious with how you use this charm in your home if you're on a flood plain; you want to work with it to repair your relationships rather than protect your home — unless of course you live on a boat and have water beneath you all the time. The ace of cups is the tarot card you should use in meditation to connect with this element.

USING THE CHARM

- Using a finger dipped in bath oil, form this symbol on the surface of a hot bath, step in and enjoy it, while thinking about having happy, fulfilling relationships with everyone in your circle of love.

- Drink plenty of water! This is not just a tip to work with this charm — too many of us forget how important water is to our health and healing. You should be aiming for a pale yellow colour in your urine when you're drinking enough water in the day.

- Writing on biodegradable paper — for example, rice paper — write this symbol in food colouring (red is good, but any colour is fine). Beneath it write a plea to Mami Wata for what you would like to have happen. Then release this paper into the sea or a running river. Do not dissolve it in stagnant water like a pond.

Charms and Symbols

The
evil eye

The idea of the evil eye dates to around 5,000 years ago. This ancient belief is based on the idea that your good fortune, good looks or happiness can attract malevolence from others. This is slightly more complicated than just the idea that someone's envious look would 'jinx' you. In fact, in some cultures, it is believed that even those who love and want the best for you can cause the evil eye to be attracted to you through unfettered love and admiration.

It is a complex idea of perfection being only the preserve of the Divine. So, in some parts of the Middle East, beautiful buildings may have a battered old pot hung in some unobtrusive corner in order for it not be too perfect and attract the evil eye. Babies and youngsters wear charms around their necks to protect them, or a parent might lick a finger and touch it behind the ears of their children — the saliva protects not just from the envious gaze of strangers but also the over-affectionate gaze of the parent.

In classical works of the Western world, the evil eye was the ability to cause harm through gaze alone, which was said to reside in certain individuals. However, in Eastern cultures, this ability is acknowledged as being more widely distributed, with anyone being able to give you the evil eye through a sudden bout of jealousy or pique. This is why charms are so often deployed to give a more general protection against a cursing look from others — whether intended or not.

You will have seen amulets featuring a blue and white circle to protect against the evil eye. These can be found on tourist items from countries such as Turkey or Egypt. In the use of such charms, the circles represent an eye that acts like a mirror and reflects the evil eye back to the sender.

Blue is traditionally used as a colour for these charms as it used to be believed that light-eyed people, who were rare in the countries where belief in the evil eye originates, could give the curse through their gaze. So, in a case of sympathetic magick, the colour is used to block the effect.

In making your own charm with this symbol, be aware that it can protect a home, possessions, a person and animals, so you can put it on virtually anything you wish to protect.

Charms and Symbols

USING THE CHARM

- A householder can have it on a hanging or painting directly opposite the front door to ensure that anyone who enters with ill intent is repelled.

- You can purchase small evil eye charms for pets to wear on their collars.

- Jewellery or keyrings are an easy way to keep the charm about your person.

THE PROTECTION OF CLOVES

Medieval parish records in England and Scotland give many instances of children or cattle having been especially affected by the evil eye. A child that has been afflicted in this way will cry for no reason, or be unusually quiet and unresponsive, sometimes with half-closed eyes. Cows will also behave unusually and may cease to give milk.

In the Indian sub-continent, the evil eye can be removed with a simple ritual involving cloves.

Take five, seven or eleven cloves, encircle the child's (or cow's) head with them in an anti-clockwise direction three times, and then burn the cloves. This removes the evil eye and the child will be back to normal shortly afterwards. If there is no smell from the burning cloves, then this is seen as a proof that it was the evil eye that had afflicted him or her.

Cloves are used in this way because it is believed that everything has a spirit and the spirit of cloves is the spirit of unseen matter. The use of cloves allows us to connect with the spirit world and warn off any evil.

The number of cloves burned is also significant in that odd numbers are considered good, while even ones are generally not. This is because when you divide even numbers into two, nothing is left, whereas with odd numbers something always remains, making them good for spellwork and prosperity.

AVOIDING THE EVIL EYE

- Horseshoes over the door of a house — ensure it is placed open side up.

- Scattering lentils in your front garden helps the birds and also repels the evil eye – urad dal (available at most Indian stores) scattered on a Saturday is particularly effective.

- Wearing an iron ring, ideally on your middle finger – this metal has a way of deflecting malevolence from all manner of entities and quarters.

- Saying a blessing from your tradition whenever you are admiring or complimenting something or someone.

- Hanging cloves in strings in your home to repel the evil eye.

- Don't strive for perfection in all things. It is sometimes good to leave a little snag of imperfection as it is said that extreme perfection or beauty can attract the evil eye.

Charms and Symbols

The
hamsa

This symbol is used throughout the Middle East and North Africa and straddles a number of different religions and cultures. Both Jewish and Muslim cultures have embraced the charm, calling it the Hand of Miriam and the Hand of Fatima respectively. Researcher Marcia Reines Josephy, writing in the mid-1980s, discovered that the use of amulets is widespread in the Reform Jewish communities of the USA where, she believed, it was seen as a symbol of good luck.

However, it seems that the original purpose of this amulet was to protect against the evil eye (see pages 96-99). It was from a protective gesture made to deflect and return the evil eye to anyone you suspected of wishing you harm. This is also why the hamsa occasionally features an eye in the palm of the hand.

The name comes from the Arabic meaning 'five', and this 'hand' is used in even very stylized forms throughout North Africa. In *The Journal of the Anthropological Institute of Great Britain and Ireland* in 1904, Edvard Westermarck wrote:

'When thus the five fingers of the hand offer protection against the dangerous look, the same must also be the case with every representation of the five fingers. In magic the difference between reality and image disappears, and little or no importance is attached to the likeness of the image. In some towns, for instance Marrakesh, there is hardly a house, and least of all a shop, on the wall or door of which the five fingers are not represented in some way or other. Sometimes you find there the rough image of a hand with outstretched fingers; sometimes only the forepart of a hand, highly conventionalized; sometimes five ' fingers' united by a horizontal line; but most commonly merely five isolated lines, longer or shorter, which occasionally dwindle almost into dots ... It is also worth noticing that in the formula which accompanies the protective gesture with the hand —'five in your eye'— the word 'finger' is not mentioned at all, only the word 'five'. The number five has thus by itself become a charm against the evil eye.'

Charms and Symbols

USING THE CHARM

You can find the hamsa on a variety of different items intended for either personal wear, such as jewellery or T-shirts, and on larger household charms like hangings and decorative plates. If painting your own, as in the section that follows, do remember the importance of the number five and feel free to make your design as stylized as you like.

- Face tattoos are probably a bit too much for most people, but the women of certain Berber tribes in North Africa wore chin tattoos affiliated with the hamsa or the palm tree. If you're feeling brave, you could try the same with temporary henna or face paint before a party to keep you protected while you are out.

- Try eating rice and lentils with your right hand — not only is this a good practice to see how other cultures eat their food, but it is also a way of connecting with your hands and remembering their importance in nourishing us.

HOW TO MAKE
A HOUSE AMULET

1. Place your own right hand on a piece of cardboard and draw around it, thus making the amulet personal to you.

2. Draw two circles within one another in the centre of the palm, to represent the eye, and decorate in colours that appeal to you.

3. Place the amulet in the entrance to your house for protection.

Your personal charm

You can also create a charm that is yours personally, not bought or even created with universal symbols – a unique object made mindfully for your own protection and fortune.

This follows one of the most important principles of magickal work, that of honing your personal power. You can only do this if you have done the energy work we looked at in part one and only once you are fully connected to the Divine energy flowing through you. Once that happens, you will find many examples of so-called 'coincidences' that come up and permit you to gain insight into what is personally protecting you and willing to help you.

It may be that a particular animal seems to be everywhere you look, or you feel a huge connection to one of your ancestors through some photos you just happen to find, or you become attracted to a certain colour more and more. It doesn't really matter too much what it is that is drawing your eye, but do look up what the traditional magickal correspondences are for those elements and see if they make sense to you.

The other important thing to remember is that energy is ever-shifting and ever-dynamic and so what works for you for a while may not do so for ever. It is vital to stay alert to your own energy movements and to avoid stagnation in your magickal work.

USING THE CHARM

Other areas to use your personal charm

- Staying safe online
- Greater wealth
- Finding love
- Mending a broken heart
- Rekindling a lapsed friendship
- Finding greater health and vitality
- Protecting your home
- Communicating with elemental spirits
  and inviting them into your garden

Charms and Symbols

FINDING YOUR CHARM

1. Find a stone or shell in a location that means something to you; it could be your garden, a local park or even an exotic beach on your holidays (although do check the local laws as some countries and areas prohibit you taking any stones or shells away with you).

2. Hold the stone (or shell) in the palm of your non-dominant hand (left, if you're right-handed, and right, if you're left-handed), close your eyes and see what images come into your mind.

3. Mentally ask the stone if it will come away with you, to help you in your life. If the answer comes back as a positive, thank the stone and take it with you. If you feel like you're getting a 'no' and the stone would prefer to stay where it is, thank it again and put it back where you found it.

4. Once you have a stone that resonates with you, you're ready to make your personal charm.

STONE CHARMS

Stone charms are inspired by thunderstones, a Haitian tradition that originates in the belief that there are powerful stones in the world that were formed during the creation of the Universe. The creation story tells of Damballah and Ayida-Wedo, the snake-gods, who gave birth to all life, during which sparks of magic fell from them as lightning to the Earth. This energy embedded itself in the landscape, producing natural places of power. Their power entered the stones in those places. That power can be accessed through painting your specific stone with intent.

When you paint your stone, you are asking the Universe to manifest that desire for you. It is deeply and profoundly personal. You then reinforce your intent each time you handle your stone. You can carry a stone made for wealth in your purse, near your wallet. A stone for getting rid of nightmares can be placed under your pillow or mattress. You can make very large charm stones for your home and garden to protect your property from theft, fire or flood. Charm stones work by helping you tap into a source of universal manifestation.

Charms and Symbols

Different types of stones

ROCKY STONES

Volcanic, jagged rocks are not usually suitable for painting but are fantastic for raising the energy in your home. If you find a particularly beautiful one, you can use it without painting it for focusing 'doing' energy into yourself. Just remember to ask the stone if it wants to come with you and, again, if it wants to be painted, if you're in any doubt.

WOODLAND STONES

These are cool, earthy stones that take on the energy of the tree canopy above them. They are very good for calming rowdy children and for helping with stress.

RIVER STONES

These stones are fantastic for healing emotional and physical wounds and calming fevers. Whatever size of your river stone, it can bring a sense of light joy into your home. Every once in a while, take your stone to running water, and wash it to renew its energy. You may even decide to paint your stone as a home protection one and pop it in your pond.

SEA STONES

These are wild, wandering stones, and you may find that these stones journey away from you after staying for a while and working their magic. They make fantastic gifts as charm stones because the more they change hands, the happier they will be. Don't worry about having an unhappy sea stone – they can find their own way back to the sea when they're finished on land.

MYSTERIOUS STONES

In the garden, in an urban pub or in your shoe, some stones turn up when you're not looking for them. Like rocky stones, these mysterious stones don't always need painting to be potent. You will know when you touch them what they're with you for. Put them on your altar or hold them when you sit in meditation – you're truly blessed if you get one.

CITY STONES

These are stones that you find in the unlikely surrounds of a teeming metropolis. They are often extra powerful because they have travelled some distance to get to you. It might even be a chip of granite with sparkly metal glinting within it.

Charms and Symbols

LOVE STONES

Throughout the world there are a number of potent symbols for love. The most ubiquitous, especially around St Valentine's Day, is the heart. Historically the heart has been regarded as the moral centre of a human being. In Egyptian mythology the heart is weighed against the feather of Maat (symbolizing truth) after a person dies. If it is heavier than the feather, it is considered to be full of sins and the person goes to hell. If it is lighter, the person is allowed to go to heaven. This may well be the origin of why we say we have a light heart when we are carefree and a heavy one when we are worried or regretful.

When exactly the heart came to be exclusively the domain of love, as opposed to morality or the intellect as it had been in the past, is unclear, but modern conceptions of romantic love would be incomplete without this symbol. We say we have a broken heart when we are crossed in love and we say we give our hearts away when we fall in love.

One symbol incorporating the heart is that of the Claddagh. This is a heart, held in two hands with a crown over it. It symbolizes love, friendship and loyalty. If you wear a Claddagh ring with the heart facing inwards towards you on your right hand, you are indicating you are in love. If you wear it outwards, you have not yet given your heart away. If you wear it on your left hand, facing inwards, your love is requited. Remember this if you decorate your spirit stone with a Claddagh and, when you meditate with your stone after you have made it, hold it facing inwards in your left hand if you wish someone you love to notice you.

People come from all over the world to south-west Ireland to kiss the Blarney Stone, which is said to bestow charm and eloquence on the kisser. Then there are the famous 'kissing' Wain Stones of the Peak District. There's so much kissing that happens with and between stones, why not ask them to help you find love? Think of the stoicism of a stone when you're getting over a broken heart. Think of the steadfastness of a stone when you're despairing of ever finding 'the one'.

PROSPERITY STONES

From coins and wheat to shamrocks, there are many symbols that are said to bring luck and prosperity. Kings have been crowned seated on stones and dragons of legend hid their treasure beneath stones. Stones with a hole worn through them by running water are considered to be exceptionally lucky fairy stones. You can paint charms to attract money and to free oneself from debt. Just look for the symbols and colours that mean prosperity to you.

HOME PROTECTION STONES

Hearth stones can be the heart of your home and are said to protect it from theft, fire and flood. People have long believed certain stones are imbued with the ability to repel evil. You can paint a charm stone up with the symbols of a happy home from the symbol for fire encased in a square (see page 90), to a key to represent your house key. Look out for the symbols that mean comfort and security at home for you.

HEALTH STONES

Many stones are said to heal people physically, from hot stone therapies to Zare Mora, a stone from the tribal regions of Balochistan in Pakistan, which was said to extract any poison from food or drink served in bowls or plates made from it. Some stones make you feel better just by holding them in your hands. Look for such stones and paint them with symbols of health, like the caduceus — a traditional sign of medical assistance.

Charms and Symbols

Painting your charm

Materials

PAINT BRUSHES

ACRYLIC PAINTS

PALETTE

QUICK-DRYING VARNISH

OLD NEWSPAPERS

Preparing your stone

Wash your stone in clean water and dry it completely. Leave it overnight in a bowl of salt, covering it entirely. In the morning, brush off the salt and take your stone to your painting space.

Sit in meditation with your stone for a while and ensure that you are meant to paint it. Some stones are very beautiful in their own right and nature has done the artistry for you. The wonderful thing about stone charms are their generosity; you can always find another stone to paint if the one that is before you is not quite right for it.

Instructions

1. Paint your base coat. This should be the colour that best corresponds to your desired outcome (see the list below). Ensure this coat dries completely before moving on to the next step. Try to keep your strokes in one direction and concentrate on your outcome as much as possible.

2. Add your pattern and symbols. This may be a two- or even three-stage process with you building up paint and patterns depending on the style you want to use. Aboriginal-inspired painting, for example, uses dots to create intricate patterns. Paint any colours on first before you use white dots to finish, ensuring you wait for each colour to dry.

3. Once all your coats of paint are dry and you are happy with your pattern, paint varnish over your stone. This will dry to a hard-wearing, glossy surface that will protect it.

Base colours to use

Love: red, pink, purple

Prosperity: green, violet, gold, silver, bronze

Home protection: blue, black, white

Health: orange, white

Charms and Symbols

Rules of

Attraction

When doing any magickal work, to ensure that you are able to attract things to you in a powerful way there are a number of things you must bear in mind. You have to practise holding a clear image of the outcome in your mind, you have to remain positive, you need to become attractive to that outcome, to deal with disappointment and, above all, practise active gratitude. This chapter addresses all of these rules.

Planes of existence

All things exist on both the material and the astral plane. To attract certain outcomes you need to influence them first on the astral plane before they can manifest on the material. This is done through energized thought. This is not true in all cases: for example, we have all created the idea of a unicorn, which exists quite happily on the astral plane; however, we have also accepted that this is a mythological beast and so the strength of that collective thought form keeps the unicorn on the astral instead of the material plane.

When you work with charms, first you are impressing upon your subconscious the reality of what you have created on the astral plane. This then manifests on the material plane to the degree that you hold the image and outcome in your mind charged with energy. If you make a charm and then treat it as something you don't think will work or have much power, that is exactly what it will become.

The most powerful magick workers are those who hold the belief in their abilities strongly and never allow doubt to enter their minds. That is chiefly the rule of attraction that we must use here. Here you will find some practices to strengthen this rule in you and your workings.

Rules of Attraction

HOW TO HOLD A STRONG IMAGE

One of the best ways to hold a strong image in your mind is to simplify it. To achieve this, follow these steps.

1. Suppose you want to protect your home. Rather than use several incantations, a number of different symbols placed around the home and a host of other protective elements, just concentrate on one thing; for example, a cord of golden light that surrounds your property and will only allow those with your best interests at heart to enter.

2. Once you have simplified the image, reinforce it by regularly meditating upon it and giving it focused energy.

3. Add practical steps towards achieving whatever it is that you are imagining coming into your life. In the case of the protected house, this may be installing a better lock or bolting the front door at night, while thinking about the energetic protection you have created.

REMAINING POSITIVE

If you are to do any protection or energy work at all, you must keep your own energy clear. This can be done using the energetic practices we looked at in part one, but as previously mentioned, you must keep your thoughts in check.

Your situation will have a great deal to do with how you think about it. If someone has betrayed you, you are financially poor or physically exhausted, your thoughts can become dominated by negative idea of want, fatigue, misery, unhappiness, loss and betrayal. However, you can change this by making a change on the astral plane. To do this you must convince your subconscious that the image you have created on the spiritual plane is more real than the one you are currently viewing on the physical plane.

One of the best ways to make this change this is to yell out (either out loud or in your mind) 'Cancel that!' the second you think or say anything negative about your situation. Then reframe what you have just said or thought in the correct way, paying attention to what you want to come to pass.

CANCEL THAT!

BEING ATTRACTIVE

Would you be attracted to you? By that I don't mean are you physically good-looking or a great romantic catch, rather are you the sort of person you would give away the last of your money simply if you were asked to do so? We all know a person like that: someone so kind, charming and sweet that they will give you the shirt off their back. If you become that person, energetically things flow to you. This can be done by watching your thoughts and words (as detailed above) and also working towards a common goal of happiness for yourself and those around you.

Let go of the ideas of want and competition and begin to express abundance and joy in everything you say and do. This can be expressed through acts of kindness to those within your sphere of influence, or it can be done more formally through donating part of your income to charities and good causes that you believe in.

In the culture I come from they say that a person has 'noor' or divine light emanating from their face when they are truly a good person. You can only be a good person through doing good deeds. Selfishness and even simple ambiguity around the idea of doing good won't attract good things to you. The astral plane can only be accessed by those who are aligned to the greater good.

Have you ever been in a situation where everything seems to just flow to you? You get three job offers instead of just one. You get money back from your tax return. The train pulls into the station just as you walk on to the platform. Every traffic light turns green as you approach it. This is called being in a state of grace and most of us only experience it for a short while and then it is gone. However, you could be in a state of grace all the time.

'OH WELL, NEXT TIME'

Do you get upset when you don't get your own way? Do you feel hard done by at being turned down for something or missing out on an award? If so you need to cultivate a relaxed attitude that meets every disappointment or denial with a cheery, 'Oh well, next time.' This is because the Universe loves grateful recipients who can nevertheless understand that not every blessing, small or large, is meant for them. Sometimes it will not be for your greater good and so you should bless whoever received it and await the greater prize that will be heading your way soon enough.

Many people might confuse this with defeatism or a lack of ambition, but this is not the case. You do still have to try for whatever it is that you want (or think you want), but you must also leave room for the divinity, the spirits or your ancestors to guide you to what is right for you. You don't know it all and arrogant insistence won't make things move any faster.

Rules of Attraction

a person has 'noor' or divine light emanating from their face when they are truly a good person

THE FIVE RULES OF ATTRACTION

1. **Gratitude** – be thankful at all times for what you already have and then you can ask for further blessings. Keep a journal or even have a diary that has extra space for entries for each day and write down all the things you're grateful for on any given day. You can always find something.

2. **Kindness** – for yourself and for others. Don't push too hard when looking for certain outcomes – you don't have to manifest the perfect life immediately. You can find 'perfect for you' bit by bit.

3. **Permission** – always ask any material you work with to help you and listen carefully with your own energy to see if permission has been given.

4. **Free will** – don't try and bend anyone else to your will. Respect that the outcome you want may not be what someone else wants and may not even be in your best interests. Always leave room for divine energy to intervene in a good way for you.

5. **Wonder** – if you feel your sense of wonder slipping away, go and look at whatever first caused you to pick up a book like this. What first sparked your interest in magick? You're not able to do magickal things if you no longer believe in magick, so keep yourself enchanted.

ACTIVE GRATITUDE

We all know that being grateful is a great way to connect with the Universe but have you ever practised active gratitude? This is where you don't just say 'Thank you' to the Universe when you get what you want – you go out and pass those blessings on. For example, suppose you did a charm for a certain amount of money to come into your life because you needed or wanted it. You visualized it well, created it on the astral plane, manifested it in reality and are now as grateful as anything. Well, take a little of that money and immediately give it to someone you think might need it. Don't worry that you will suddenly not have enough; this principle is one of growth and not limitation. Even if you have a large debt and have only manifested a quarter of the amount, take a little and either buy a small gift for someone you know is having a hard time, or put it in a charity box. You can also do something really magical like putting it in a library book or down the side of a train seat so that it can find its way to someone by sheer 'luck' alone. It may not reach a very desperate person but it might ignite a belief in luck and magick in someone who needs to know that we are all protected by a divine source.

DON'T GIVE UP

Finally, there is a tendency to give up on your wish, just as it is about to manifest. If you heard the expression that 'the darkest hour is just before the dawn', then this should be a guiding principle for you. Whenever things start to look very glum, redouble your efforts of faith, good thoughts and deeds. Rather than sob into your pillow and curse your fate, go and do something practical and productive towards your end goal. If that is to get a job, see if one of your friends can help you review your resumé and make it better. If it is to get more money, check to see if you can monetize a hobby. You will find that the more you work to impress your subconscious of the truth you want to bring forth, the easier things will get. And when your full manifestation takes place, you will feel vindicated and delighted and all the hard work will seem an age away.

Results and recharging

Within alchemy there is indeed a fifth element in addition to the four that we looked at as protection charms in the last section (see pages 88-95). That fifth element is spirit or ether. It is the space that permits the other elements to work. And here is the crazy bit — the fifth element is you.

In order for your elemental — or indeed any — charms to work, you must also keep the fifth element that is *you* in tip-top condition. This is done primarily through good nutrition and adequate rest. A lot of people don't appreciate the importance of this and they add magickal work as an addition to their to-do list, running on empty until they collapse.

If you find that your protection charms or any other spellwork are not working, your first port of call should be to recharge yourself. Once a year, for a whole month, I stop all spiritual practice. This is not because I cease to believe or that the spirit somehow takes a holiday from my life. It is that the body needs recharging and renewal. I place a black velvet cloth over my altar. I cease my morning meditation and, if I can afford it, I even take myself off on holiday to break entirely from my routine. I don't disappear for the whole month — few of us have that luxury — but I do ensure that I am in 'holiday mode' even on the days that I am going to work and coming home. I catch up on non-magic culture: boxsets of crime dramas; literary fiction; dare I say it, reality TV shows.

Now, it isn't that I never consume any of that sort of culture during the other eleven months of the year. It is more that I am in a conscious manifesting phase during that time, and I tend to find myself attracted to things that help me in what I want to happen. Strange coincidences, meeting the right person at the right time, books that solve a problem for me, and TV that clarifies situations for me. Do you recall at the beginning of this book that I said everyone is unique and individual and so what works for me might not do so for you? Well, this is a great example of that.

ENERGY RENEWAL

My father is an energy healer and he often sees many clients in a given day. I remember asking him why he didn't seem exhausted at the end of his working day. He explained that when the energy comes through him to heal others, some of it leaks into his system and so the more he heals, the more he benefits from it himself. This was interesting to hear because it is actually precisely the opposite for my work.

Spellwork and manifestation is tiring because the energy used, while charged by Divine energy, requires some physical, manifested heavy lifting. To work with different energies and blend them smoothly takes effort. To engage in certain occult practices is energetically demanding and can be exhausting. It took me twenty years before I realized that the way I could recharge my work and make sure it was still effective was to have this time off.

In fact, initially I took a whole two years off entirely. Those were unhappy years as I did feel disconnected from my greater purpose. However, it allowed me to consolidate my energy, learn a few hard lessons about gratitude and productive ways of thinking, and finally it allowed me to return to magick with my faith renewed and my bonds to divinity stronger than ever.

Over time I finessed my situation down to understanding exactly when and how I should renew my energy, and now I take the month of December off. I do follow a pagan calendar, so it does mean that the Saturnalia or Yule celebrations that I engage in are less to do with spiritual connection and more to do with partying.

HOW TO REPLENISH YOUR LIFE FORCE

When you begin to feel tired and unmotivated to do any magickal work, it may be that you need to replenish your energy. Here is what you should do at such times.

1. Think back to a time when you felt perfectly happy. Was it lying on a beach feeling the sun on your face? The first time you kissed your partner? Holding your baby for the first time? Think hard about what experience represents a 'peak moment' in your life.

2. Consider how you can get back some of that feeling right now, today. Could you go home and relax in a hot bath, pretending like you're in a warm sea at night? Could you kiss your partner again as if it were the very first time, connecting deeply and igniting the same excitement? Could you spend some mindful moments with your child, even if he or she is no longer a baby, and cuddle them?

3. Remember the things that make you happy and do them more often. There is nothing more complicated than that to renewing your energy.

Finally, remember that variety is important in life so, even if you're most happy at your desk at work, you need to have time off or the 'sameness' of your days will begin to suck away your energy — even if you think you're mostly happy. Mix it up a bit!

Your personality energy make-up

Let's start to find out how your energy works. Answer the questions that follow as honestly as possible.

Extrovert or Introvert?

WOULD YOU DESCRIBE YOURSELF AS AN EXTROVERT OR AN INTROVERT?

Thinking deeply about these questions, consciously try and be/do the opposite for a limited space of time, such as a month. So, if you're an introvert, try to go out and meet new people. If you're an extrovert, stay in and try to hibernate. If you feel tired after you've been in the company of others, avoid them for a while. If you feel fine, fresh and renewed, try seeing some more people and note afterwards how you are feeling. If you start to flag, after how many such meetings in a month does this happen — three, four, six? Really pay attention to how you feel after socializing.

Commit to Yourself

DO YOU OFTEN 'FORGET' OR MISS YOUR MEDITATIONS OR SPECIFIC SPIRITUAL PRACTICES THAT YOU'VE SAID YOU WANT TO DO?

If you keep forgetting your meditations, commit to spending a month religiously doing them. Set a timer if you need to or perhaps select some music that might help you sustain the practice. How do you feel after each meditation? Do you feel resentful? Tired? Better afterwards or irritated? Note down these thoughts and feelings in your journal and see if you feel differently at the end of the month than you did at the beginning.

Active or Inactive?

HOW PHYSICALLY ACTIVE ARE YOU?

If you're a couch potato, book yourself in for a month of physically demanding classes like Zumba or circuit training. If you're a very physically active person, try to slow down for a month, doing nothing other than the bare minimum. Note how you feel. Did the exercise make you feel ill and angry? Or did you feel invigorated and proud of yourself for going? What about if you're usually active and you have had a month of doing very little. Did that make you feel sick and frustrated? Where you anxious to get back to the gym as soon as the month was over? Or could you happily do another month of just chilling? Did you completely ignore these suggestions and stick to your usual routine (which is also fine)?

In noting these reactions, you will start to build up a picture of how you like to be in the world. If your personality and energetic make-up is that of a physically active extrovert, then you need to develop practices that match this. You may work well within a group or coven that do quite physical rituals once a month and create your protection charms as part of that. Get online and find your people. If you are a more of an introvert, perhaps you need a more meditative way of staying healthy, such as yoga, and your magick might be better if you are solitary and away from other people.

Spellwork

WHAT FEELING DO
YOU GET WHEN YOU
BEGIN SOME SPELLWORK,
WHETHER THAT IS MAKING
PROTECTIVE CHARMS OR ANY
OTHER SUCH PRACTICE?

Finally, the most important question of all — how did you feel just
before doing magickal work? The answer to this question will let
you know whether this is your time to be doing work like this. If
you feel apprehensive or bored, like you're doing a chore, not
only will your magick be weak, it will also be an irritant in
your life. Leave it all aside for a while until you get that
little pull of wonder and excitement again.

Altars

Altars are not just religious arrangements; they are increasingly used by people to create a beautiful focus for their daily meditations. I am a huge advocate of altars, because I believe that a visual, physical place to focus your energy makes your magick work better, and they are just things of beauty. The interest in subjects such as feng shui and vastu shastra, which focus on the arrangement of homes to ensure the correct flow of energy, has also led some to experiment with using altars as manifestation tools. This means that you can create altars that bring love or money into your life; it's simply a matter of identifying where in your home you could set up a suitable altar for love or material abundance, and what to put on it.

There is a huge depth of variety when creating an altar. You can use all the senses to make a really special tool for focusing the mind. Your sense of sight can take in beautiful colours and objects; you can smell sweet incense and aromatic smoke; you can partake of delicious offerings that you share with the deity or spirit to whom you have dedicated your altar; and you can place a bell, singing bowl or wind chime before your altar that can transport you to another space and time. By placing tactile objects like stones and shells on your altar, you can also use your sense of touch to lose yourself in the patterns of the Universe. In short, your altar is a place of stimulation, where you connect with the greater life of the Universe and all that is part of it.

Creating your altar is a meditative process and here I will show you how to find special objects for your altar by questing for them.

SETTING UP YOUR ALTAR

1. Begin by walking through your home looking for a place that would be perfect for your altar. Don't just look for practical things, such as space on a shelf or mantel, or the room that is the least used.

2. Look also for how the space *feels*. As you develop your magickal skills, you should be able to feel the energy of an area of a room and know whether this is an appropriate place for your altar. My altar is very low down and counterintuitive to where you would expect an altar to be. My father was surprised by it as within his tradition, you never put anything sacred near the feet. Holy books and devotional prayer beads are all kept above the waist level and ideally above the head. This is because the head is where divine energy first enters your body. However, in my tradition, every part of the body is sacred and equally connected to the Divine. Therefore, I am perfectly as ease kneeling at an altar that is virtually on the floor.

3. Once you have found the space you will use, you must clean it thoroughly. If it is a shelf, don't just wipe it down, check what is below it and behind it and ensure that there are no hidden cobwebs or dust there either.

4. Then, using one of the methods described on page 42, energetically clean the space as well.

FOCUS

To begin setting up your altar, you must first select the focus. This is an object that sits at the heart of your altar. It will help if you take a look through the elements charms on pages 88-95 and think about which element attracts you the most. You may find that the element connected with your Sun sign is the strongest for you.

For a focus that is linked to the element of fire, place a fireproof cauldron or bowl in the centre of your altar. For water, a bowl of water. For earth, a bowl of earth or a plant. For air, you can choose a feather or the same as for fire since air feeds fire.

Once you have placed your chosen item at the centre of your altar, take a deep breath in and out through your nose and then settle down in meditation in front of your altar. During your meditation, state your intent to use this altar to channel your energy and aid your magickal work. Thank the Divine energy for enabling you to do this work for the good of yourself and those around you.

Fire:

ARIES

LEO

SAGITTARIUS

Water:

CANCER

SCORPIO

PISCES

Earth:

TAURUS

VIRGO

CAPRICORN

Air:

GEMINI

LIBRA

AQUARIUS

QUESTING

We tend not to go on quests or pilgrimages much nowadays. I know some still do worldwide, but in the West we are much more likely to go away for two weeks to get a bit of holiday sun than we are to visit holy shrines and places considered centres of sacred learning.

One of the ways to create a powerful altar is to quest for the items that you will place on it. This can be as simple as taking a walk in a local park with the intention of finding a gift from the Universe to place on your altar, or it could be a once-in-a-lifetime trip to a place that resonates with you, such as the pyramids in Egypt or Uluru in Australia to find insights and possibly a souvenir that you can place on your altar to remind you of the feeling you had during your visit. Please be very conscious of not taking away anything that you are legally or spiritually forbidden. A tourist trinket that is a representation of the majesty you saw there is a hundred times better than a large fine or the disapproval of the spirits of a place.

Before you make your journey, sit in meditation in front of your altar and ask to be shown a sign for what to bring back to this point of focus and attention. Sometimes, you will be gifted something without intending it or questing for it, and it is wonderful when that happens, but if you can plan a specific trip for this purpose, it will be very energetically charged.

If you have dedicated your altar to a specific type of energy or particular deity, you should be aware of what is sacred to that entity. Volcanic rock is good to place on a fire elemental altar. A sea pebble is good for one that is dedicated to a marine deity such as Mami Wata. Read as much as you can about the symbols, objects, colours and other associations linked to the god or goddess or energy you are working with. You can also link your altar to a deity by buying or making two sets of objects — for example, two protection charms. Place one ritualistically on your altar and carry out a ritual at the right place and time with the other. The two will then be linked and charge each other. Opposite is an example of that.

MAMI WATA OFFERING

Ross Heaven, author and shamanic practitioner, taught me a powerful practice for connecting with the ocean mother goddess Yemaya or Mami Wata. She is the goddess of love and is often depicted in the form of a beautiful mermaid. She is particularly helpful when petitioned to resolve relationship problems and can also offer blessings of prosperity and fertility.

1. On the night of a full moon, make an offering parcel in biodegradable paper. You can include sweet foods, a tot of rum, some incense, a little edible glitter and anything else that seems appropriate (nothing plastic that may harm sea life). Include the second protection charm in your parcel.

2. Write a list of what you would love to have happen over the coming year and thank Mami Wata for her help. Put that in with the offering, too.

3. Tie up the bundle with natural string; don't worry if it's a little damp due to the rum.

4. If you live by the sea, take it down to the water's edge, preferably at night-time (but be safety conscious), and gently release it into the sea. Running water like a river will do if you don't live by the sea. Remember don't throw it into the water, as you are making an offering, not disposing of litter!

Traditionally the belief is that if the parcel washes back up on the shore your wishes will not be granted on this particular occasion, but if the parcel is carried out to sea, you should see your hopes fulfilled — possibly before the next full moon.

Rules of Attraction

State of
attraction

Charms, as I mentioned earlier, are often used in conjunction with spoken words. Sitting at your altar, you too can charge your protection charm with your words. It does not need to be an ancient charm said in Hebrew or Latin! You can simply state what you want the charm to protect you against, be that poverty, loneliness or a threat to your home.

Through these two methods — visual, using a physical charm, and verbal, through the spoken charm — you can set in motion a state of attraction that allows protective energies to flow towards you.

Always remember to frame your charms positively. So instead of, 'I no longer attract abusive men' for a love protection charm, you should say 'I attract loving, supportive relationships'. Instead of, 'I am no longer poor', it would be, 'I am rich financially and in all other ways'. A charm is essentially an affirmation for which you are applying to universal energy, so the same principles apply. When you're connecting with a specific deity, you add in a petition: 'I humbly ask Mami Wata to bring me wealth and happiness'; 'I honour lady Venus and ask that she make me a vehicle of her beauty and grace.'

PERSONAL GROOMING

This is a touchy subject for me as I am incredibly lazy. I tend to just shower in the morning and then look upon the epic beauty regime of my sister with shock and awe. Some people spend an inordinate amount of time, money and energy on looking good. I applaud them for it since I have neither the mental nor the financial resources for that level of grooming. However, if you are to remain in a state of attraction, you must follow a personal grooming regime. This is because you are signalling that you are ready for some changes.

This can simply be ensuring you look and feel your best if you've begun dating again after some time, or it can be nourishing your soul with gorgeous-smelling baths to indicate that you are worthy of pampering. As odd as it may seem in a book on magickal protection charms, people can forget that they are the main conduit through which divinity flows.

Archaeologists have found all manner of items of personal grooming and hygiene dating back to Neolithic times, making this a concern for us as human beings. However, it has also been a part of spiritual rituals for as long as we have had religions. We bathe and put on our 'Sunday best' to go to church. We have ablutions before going in to pray. We prepare our bodies for big life events such as weddings and birthing. In the same way, we must keep up a way of reminding ourselves that we are important and that we honour the work that we are doing.

How you do this is entirely personal to you – it is not called 'personal' grooming for nothing. You may be a natural eco-warrior who makes her own deodorant or you may love luxury facials and waxing treatments. Only you can decide what works for you, but stay conscious of this as a part of being in a state of attraction.

Rules of Attraction

Energetic
blockages

We may find we experience energy blockages. This can be for a number of reasons. Here we identify what these might be and how we can work to address them.

Certain substances such as alcohol and coffee can cause energetic blockages; this is not because they are bad *per se*, it is more that they ground you in the physical rather than allowing you to flow into the spiritual. It is always best to have your morning coffee after your morning meditation. You will float far more easily into the spiritual realm and then the grounding with your morning cup will feel even more welcome and delicious.

ADDICTIONS

Addictions are problematic for more than just reasons of ill health and unhappiness. They cause a block in your energetic channels that make it more difficult to connect with the source of all life. You're never disconnected, but it can start to feel that way because those channels are so sluggish. You also find it harder and harder to attract the right things to you.

Your connection to the divine source of all energy is never broken, no matter how much it might feel on occasion; it is just that it can get clogged by negativity, a poor belief system and guilt over things you may have said and done. This then causes you to make unhealthy choices with regard to what you put in your body. It is only by clearing that channel of those blockages that you open yourself up again to a free flow of Divine energy that can release a wonderful creative force in your life.

THOUGHTS

What causes us to slip out of that state of grace, where we're attracting the best to us? Our thoughts. We loop around, thinking about what we lack and forget about what we already have that is good. We wonder if we're doing the work we're meant to do, if we will ever find our soulmate, when we will enjoy good health, how we will again get the sense of wonder and connection with nature we felt as children. All is possible, this and more, but you need to commit to giving time to clearing your energy and doing some manifestation work once that has been done.

Police your thoughts for the next few weeks and make a conscious note of when you are thinking something that is making you feel unhappy. How often do you have a complaint or a criticism? Nothing knocks us out of a state of attraction quicker than judging or criticizing the world around us. You may think the two things are not related. You're criticizing your boss in your mind, but that's okay because you only want to manifest a new partner, not a new boss, so what harm can it do if you think he's a fool? It hurts because the mechanism through which you are manifesting does not know the difference. It also doesn't know the difference between you and other people. So criticism of someone else is criticism of the self.

This can seem a bit difficult to understand at first, and nobody can be a Pollyanna the whole day long, and never say or think anything horrible about anyone. But you must guard against it if you can. If you find yourself thinking something awful about someone, think something nice about them straight away. So, if you're annoyed that someone bumped into you on the pavement and you think they are a clumsy idiot, see if there is something nice you can say about them. Great choice of outfit, perhaps? Excellent walking pace? I know it is hard, but do try it. You're helping yourself as much as the other person.

FEAR

Finally, another way to knock yourself out of a state of attraction is to give in to fear. It doesn't matter what you are afraid of, and sometimes it won't even look much like fear. Fear of failure often manifests itself as simply not trying rather than quivering in the wings. Fear of rejection can mean we never ask for anything. (And as we all know, if you don't ask, you don't get.) Fear of the future can stagnate us in the past and result in a refusal to change anything. None of these types of fear are helpful to us, but they are rooted in protection. We are trying to protect ourselves from pain and hurt. The way to deal with this fear is to coax yourself in the way you would a fearful child. One would hope you wouldn't yell at them and tell them to stop being so silly. You would gently try and show them that there is nothing to be afraid of - no bogeyman under the bed, no monsters in the cupboard. You can ask yourself - what's the worst that could happen? Being laughed at is not fatal. Being told 'No, thank you' does not mean you are unlovable. Having to move on in life doesn't mean you can never appreciate the past.

Treat yourself with compassion and go as slowly as you need to in order to get to where you want to be. Take baby steps. If your fear is around taking risks in your career, start small. Perhaps take an evening class in the area you'd like to move into rather than giving up your job in one big terrifying move. To paraphrase President Franklin D. Roosevelt, you have nothing to fear but fear itself.

Situations

When going about your everyday life, you will encounter situations where you need extra help, where you want to be able to call upon a higher power to support you. I carry a protection charm with me in my pocket at all times so that at times like this I can simply hold it in my hand, very discreetly, and know that I am under an umbrella of protection.

In order to properly predict when you might need some extra help, have a think about what you're excited about. Are you looking forward to an event such as a party or holiday that you know you will really enjoy? What are you dreading? Is there a person or event that fills you with apprehension and anxiety? Most of us, even if we're not feeling it right now, can remember times that we have felt very happy and excited about a forthcoming event and, conversely, we can also recall stressful situations that we would have chosen to avoid if we could have done so. Life is punctuated with such moments and how we prepare or react to them is a good indication of whether our magickal work is doing its thing.

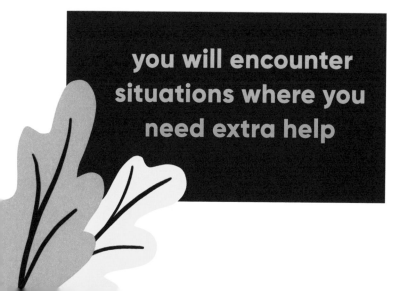

you will encounter situations where you need extra help

LIST IT OUT

Make a list of all the situations where you feel uncomfortable. These could be situations that other people find enjoyable, such as dates or going to the cinema. After you have made your list, write after each one why you should put yourself in that situation. So, for example, if you have written 'dating', you would put that you want to meet someone and have a meaningful romantic relationship. However, if your only reason for dating is that your mum wants grandchildren, you may need to remove that situation from your life temporarily (or for ever if it's just not your thing — remember, just because Hollywood or our parents tell us something is 'normal' and we *should* want it, doesn't mean we *have* to or that it is 'normal' for us).

....

....

....

....

....

....

....

....

....

....

Your list will show you where you need help and where you want to be focusing your energetic manifestation work. If you put 'networking events' on your list and the reason is that you want to be a key player in your industry, and you genuinely want that, then this is a great place to pour some energy. Ensuring you are in a state of attraction (see pages 138–139), begin to look for symbols and signs associated with success and connection: two hands clasped in a deal-making handshake; dollar sign for prosperity; an arrow pointing upwards as it would on a business growth chart.

You can also look for deities connected with good business. For example, the elephant-headed Hindu god Ganesha is seen as the remover of obstacles. Certain animals are also connected with commerce: the Bambara people of Mali believe that agriculture was taught to them by the antelope, so a farmer might want to use antelopes in the charms she uses.

You can then create a charm specifically for a given situation. Take it with you on a networking night and give it a little rub for luck before you walk into the event. The energy you have put into the situation and preparing for it will help you.

Rules of Attraction

EMERGENCY CHARMS

We have seen how charms can be verbal or written or objects with symbols on them. Sometimes you won't have time to do a more involved ritual, find symbols and create a protection charm. You may be on your way home alone and something about the person walking behind you is making you feel nervous. Or your heart is pounding because you've been asked, at the last minute, to present your ideas in a meeting. You can keep an emergency protection charm under your belt for just such an occasion: 'Protect me from harm, Divine Beloved.' You can say it, mouth it, think it, trace it on your hand with your finger. You can use it in a variety of different ways, completely discreetly.

The greater your connection through other practices at less urgent times, the more this will spring into action when you need it. I once saw a documentary that said that the more positive the news a society watched, the less afraid it was and fewer crimes were committed. Certainly, when I was in Ireland, where both the population and the crime levels are lower than in the UK, I noticed how much of the news concentrated on good stories over bad ones. Generally speaking, even the national news programmes were shocked by, and debated at length, stories that would have just been a normal Saturday-night occurrences in some parts of London. It made me feel safer and I imagine it must have had a similar effect on the people living in Ireland.

If you possibly can, try and keep what you see and hear towards the positive. Obviously, that won't always be possible, but one way of keeping yourself protected is to think well of the world around you. If you constantly feed yourself on a diet of how terrible human beings can be, you will start to expect that behaviour of the people you encounter. Conversely, if you tend towards thinking that most people are lovely, you will expect them to be nice to you. In both cases, you will find that people rarely disappoint.

STRANGER DANGER

We have looked at how honing your intuition will help you avoid danger in everyday life. However, if you're walking the streets and you suddenly feel uncomfortable about a situation – for example, you're walking towards some young people who are loud and sound aggressive – immediately imagine a golden shield going up and out from the point of your belly and becoming an impenetrable golden bubble around you. Then walk confidently through the crowd, remembering how much fun it was to be a young teenager swearing and hanging out with your friends when parents weren't about. Most people are harmless and do not want to hurt you.

Rules of Attraction

**protect me from harm,
Divine Beloved**

EVERYDAY IRKSOME

The shop assistant who is being actively grumpy and unhelpful. The bus driver who pulls away despite you running like mad to make it to the stop in time. The person who jolts you on the train and doesn't bother apologizing. There are so many petty irritations out there in the world, but that's precisely what they are: petty. They aren't big enough to affect you. Whenever you feel as though you're about to lose your cool, say in your mind (or out loud if you're feeling brave): 'I forgive you and I bless you.' You don't know the agonies someone else might be going through, so don't assume they were just born awful.

DEMANDING BOSSES

Whether a bully or someone unrealistic in their demands, nothing can put a spanner in your day like a bad boss. As with any magickal work, first check if there is anything practical you can do about your boss. Can you ask for a meeting where you raise your concerns? Can you set boundaries for how you work? In extreme cases, can you get another job? If none of those are options, bless a bowl of Florida water (you can find it in any shop selling Caribbean goods), sprinkle it around your desk, imagining that it is creating a barrier of protection through which none can cross.

ONLINE TROLLS

First things first, get offline. Immediately. Even if you have to unplug and disconnect from your network, you must immediately stop being online. This is vital. Not one last comment. One last trying to get the last word in. Go take a handful of any salt you like and go to the bathroom and rub it across your belly. Imagine there is a golden light where the salt has touched. Then, at least 24 hours later, go back to where you found the troll and block them, deleting any comments they may have added in the interim, ideally without reading them.

If it is a friend or family member who has made you feel unsafe or unhappy online, leave social media for a week or so and then see if you still feel as strongly about what was said. If you do, you are perfectly within your rights to block friends and family as well.

SELF-SABOTAGE

Do you regularly do things that you then beat yourself up about because it was against your interest? Dating the wrong guys. Procrastinating until pressure builds. Messing up at your dream job? This can often stem from a fear of success. Yes, you read right, a fear of... success, and not failure. We often self-sabotage because we don't know what we'd do with ourselves if we succeeded. We fear the jealousy of others. We fear that we would not be able to sustain the success. We fear the gods punish the fortune. Nonsense! Have no fea — the gods love us and always have. If you sense yourself about to do something counter to your best interests, imagine that you are protecting a young child — your child. What decision would you make to secure that child's future and happiness? Visualize the little one you are about to save and make your decisions from that place of protectiveness and wisdom.

Hatches, matches and despatches

'Hatch, match and despatch' is a humorous way to describe the three main times of life you may need extra help in the form of protection charms. Babies always need extra protection to ensure a smooth birth for both mother and child, and then a healthy, robust childhood for the wee 'hatchling'. Weddings can be a stressful time, with expectations and fears running high, so we want to create some comfort and reassurance in the run-up to the big day. Then there are rituals around death to ensure the safe passage of the soul of loved ones to the afterlife, but also to heal the people who are left behind.

Depending on your belief system, you can use angelic sigils, universal shapes, or even sit in meditation and find your own symbols that arise when you think about an upcoming event. It can be lovely to make a charm for a friend or family member, but always ask permission first as the person you are making it for may not want something that doesn't fit in with their belief system. Don't be offended if the answer is a 'no' — consent is one of the most important parts of living together in the world, and we should all be wary of forcing our beliefs onto others.

CHARMS FOR SPECIFIC EVENTS

- **Births** – if you have permission for it, it can be a great thing to sew particular charms into a baby blanket. This then becomes a wonderful heirloom that will be treasured for years once the baby is all grown up.

- **Weddings** – if the wedding party is receptive, you can consider making personal charms as part of the hen or stag do. A bit of crafting earlier in the day (for example, painting stones or carving wooden amulets) can create a shared bond that makes the celebrations later in the evening go really well.

- **Funerals** – a small stone or clover from near the grave of a loved one can be painted or pressed into a book and made into a remembrance charm to bring comfort when you are grieving.

- **Other times of need**

  ▸ A job search and/or interview can go better if you write exactly what you want to feel in your new job on a small piece of paper and wear it in a locket around your neck. You will energetically tell the Universe what you want to manifest.

  ▸ If you're heading out to a party and are nervous about speaking to new people, consider wearing a blue scarf or ribbon as a charm around your neck to open up your throat chakra and make communication easier.

  ▸ If you're feeling a bit run-down and have already been checked out by a medical professional, then consider drawing out the symbol for Mars and taping it to a clear water bottle. Use filtered water in the bottle and see if this increases your energy levels. If you find that you're getting into more disputes, add the symbol for Venus next to it to balance out the energies.

A final note

You should now be equipped to create a whole range of protection charms according to your own intuition and research into each area in which you want to manifest protection. You may now have a beautiful collection of amulets gathered as gifts, purchases and vintage finds. You may have created a gorgeous altar at which you can do your daily meditations. However, don't forget that energy is an endlessly moving river, with currents and eddies that move through you moment by moment. Energy cannot be solidified into one charm or amulet for ever more. Not even the most impressive magickian can make that happen.

An amulet or charm is only as powerful as the person imbuing it with power. Their ability to focus and draw down Divine energy and place it into an object is what makes it powerful. If the creation is done half-heartedly, the amulet won't work. Oddly enough, in the past, I have known of talisman-makers who have failed in creating a talisman of efficacy because they got their maths wrong — the magic square technique requires a certain degree of prowess with numbers.

Once you have created your protection charm, don't leave it languishing at the bottom of your bag or dusty on your altar. When you sense that the energy is starting to go from an amulet, you can do one of two things — you can either recharge it or send it on its way.

Amulets and charms aren't jewellery and I would never treat them as such. They are sacred objects of power with a job to do. How annoyed would you be if someone hired you to do a job and then asked you just to sit at your desk doing nothing but looking pretty? I'm fairly sure the employment lawyers would be called. Your charm is no different. Use it or let it go and be useful to others.

You can sell on particularly valuable vintage charms and amulets. If it is one you made yourself from a stone, you should put it back into running water or bury it where it won't be disturbed.

Alternatively, you can recharge it by leaving it overnight in a bowl of salt and then sitting in meditation with it the next day, re-consecrating it to its purpose. You will know how often you should do that by the energy the charm emits.

I hope you will find great success with the techniques outlined in this book. It is my wish for you that the Divine Source of All Things protect you from harm, always.

Further
reading

Journals

Biroco, Joel. *KAOS*. www.biroco.com/kaos/index.html

Bonner, Campbell. 'Magical Amulets', *The Harvard Theological Review*, Vol. 39, No. 1 (Jan. 1946), pp. 25–54. www.jstor.org/stable/1507999

'Witchcraft Casebook: Magic in Russia, Ukraine, Poland, and the Grand Duchy of Lithuania, 15th–21st Centuries' *Russian History*, Vol. 40, No. 3/4 (2013), pp. 532–539.

Books

Ball, Pamela J. *Spells, Charms, Talismans and Amulets*. Arcturus, 2001.

Eason, Cassandra. *Complete Book of Spells*. Quantum, 2004.

Heaven, Ross. *Vodou Shaman: The Haitian Way of Healing and Power*. Destiny Books, 2003.

Illes, Judika. *The Element Encyclopedia of 5000 Spells*. Element, 2004.

Kahili King, Serge. *Mastering Your Hidden Self: A Guide to the Huna Way*. Quest, 1996.

Nozedar, Adele. *The Illustrated Signs and Symbols Sourcebook*. Harper Collins Publishers, 2016.

Shah, Idries. *Oriental Magic*. ISF Publishing, 2019.

Wallis Budge, E. A. *Egyptian Magic*. Chartwell, 2016.

Website

www.astro.com

Index

Glossary

Alchemy: An ancient philosophy concerned with changing base metals into gold and transforming the spirit in a similar way.

Amulets: A protective object that can be worn or put up at home.

Axis mundi: The point of connection between the Earth, the underworld and the heavens.

Ayida-Wedo: A spirit or god of fertility in the Vodou tradition, wife to Damballah.

Bulla: An amulet given to male children in ancient Rome.

Chakras: Centres of energy in the body, first written about in the ancient texts of India, and since developed into various systems by energetic healers.

Charms: Verbal or written protective phrases and objects intended to protect the person saying the charm or wearing it.

Curse-speak: Negative thoughts and phrases, sometimes through genuine concern or worry. For example, a mother being worried that her child will fall saying 'Be careful, you'll fall!'

Damballah: The creator god of all life in the Vodou tradition, husband to Ayida-Wedo.

Divine/Universal energy: The universal energy that flows through everything and everyone.

Egun: The spirits of departed ancestors in the Yoruba tradition.

Gnostic: First century AD Christian and Jewish ideas and works that emphasized spiritual knowledge over dogma.

Hamsa: The hand symbol from North Africa and the Middle East that is used as a protective charm against the evil eye by both Jewish and Muslim communities.

Kali: The Indian goddess who is a great protector and considered mother of all the world.

Karma: Our experiences over all our life cycles.

Kyranides: Magickal texts in Greek compiled in the 4th century.

Mami Wata: Water spirit venerated in the Vodou tradition, often depicted as a mermaid.

Naf: Both the belly button and the position on the torso where the centre of a person's spiritual/ emotional energy lies.

Ofuro: The word for a Japanese bath and the ritual of bathing.

Onsen: Japanese word for hot springs where communal, daily bathing takes place.

Ouroboros: The snake biting its own tail, a powerful, mystical symbol of infinity.

Prometheus: The Titan who made humans from clay and gave us the gift of fire, for which he was punished by Zeus, king of the gods of Olympus.

Sansenoy: One of the three angels in charge of medicine that are said to be a protection against the demon Lilith. The other two are Semangelof and Senoy

Santeria: A religion of Yoruba origin that developed in Cuba from its West African roots.

Sekhmet: Protective Egyptian warrior goddess, depicted with the head of a lioness.

Semangelof: One of the three angels in charge of medicine that are said to be a protection against the demon Lilith. The other two are Sansenoy and Senoy.

Senoy: One of the three angels in charge of medicine that are said to be a protection against the demon Lilith. The other two are Sansenoy and Semangelof.

Shakti: Divine feminine energy.

Shamanism: The practice of communicating with the spirits through altered states of consciousness.

Shiv: Also, Shiva, Indian god, also known as The Destroyer, who is the Lord of Divine Energy. Also divine male energy.

Smudging: Energetically cleansing a space through the burning of herb bundles, often made from sage.

Sri Yantra: The mystical Hindu diagram believed to represent aspects of the great goddess with nine layers or levels of meaning.

Sufism: A mystical Islamic tradition that transcends sects and emphasises spiritual unity with God.

Tantric: Pertaining to the mystical traditions of Hinduism and Buddhism and the rituals and practices given in that complex philosophy.

Tawiz: An amulet containing a charm that references verses from the Quran.

Titan: The twelve children of the Sky and Earth in Greek mythology who predated the Olympian gods and their progeny.

Yemaya: The goddess worshipped in the Yoruba tradition, linked with and often synonymous with Mami Wata in Vodou practice.

Yoruba: A distinct group of people of West Africa and the traditions and spirituality of that culture.

Zagovory: Russian verbal folk magick including spoken charms and enchantments.

Glossary

Acknowledgements

Thank you to Lisa Dyer, Severine Jeaneau, Nicolette Kaponis, Abi Read, Katie Hewett, Chloe Moss and all the team at Eddison Books for commissioning this book and putting it together so beautifully.

Thanks to Claire Gillman for supporting my writing by giving me a column in *Kindred Spirit* magazine – I wish I adulted as well as you do.

Thanks also to my parents for always protecting me energetically and with the use of that most potent of talismans – their love.

Thank you to the late, great Ross Heaven, and the writers and researchers who taught me so much about this subject.

Finally, thank you to Gary for putting up with the endless whining that always accompanies me getting a book written.